IF THE TONGUE'S A FIRE, WHO NEEDS SALSA?

If the Tongue's a Fire, Who Needs Salsa?

Cool Advice for Hot Topics From the Book of James

MARTHA BOLTON

SERVANT PUBLICATIONS
ANN ARBOR, MICHIGAN

Vine Books is an imprint of Servant Publications especially designed to serve evangelical Christians.

Servant Publications—Mission Statement
We are dedicated to publishing books that spread the gospel of Jesus Christ, help Christians to live in accordance with that gospel, promote renewal in the church, and bear witness to Christian unity.

Unless otherwise indicated all Scripture quotations are from the Holy Bible, New International Version, copyright 1973, 1978, 1984 by International Bible Society. Used by permission of Zondervan Publishing House. All rights reserved.

Published by Servant Publications
P.O. Box 8617
Ann Arbor, Michigan 48107
www.servantpub.com

Cover design: PAZ Design Group, Salem, Oreg.
Cover illustration: Pat Binder

02 03 04 05 10 9 8 7 6 5 4 3 2 1

Printed in the United States of America
ISBN 1-56955-318-1

Library of Congress Cataloging-in-Publication Data

Bolton, Martha, 1951-
    If the tongue's a fire, who needs salsa? : cool advice for hot
topics from the book of James / Martha Bolton.
        p. cm.
    ISBN 1-56955-318-1 (alk. paper)
    1. Bible. N.T. James–Devotional literature. 2. Christian teenagers–Prayer-books
and devotions–English.   I. Title.
    BS2785.54.B65 2002
    242'.63–dc21

                                                                    2002008218

To Reverend Bob Reith

for his friendship,
his wisdom,
his love and encouragement,
and for all that he does for so many.

Contents

Acknowledgments

Thank you to:

My husband, Russ, for always being right by my side through every twist and turn of this life.

Russ II, Matt, Tony, Crystal, Nicole, Kiana, Kadin, and Lily. Never ever forget how much God loves you.

To Kathy Deering, Bert Ghezzi, Don Cooper, and everyone at Vine Books for being so wonderful to work with, and a special thank you to Sandy Judd for always keeping me on track with my deadline (and for being so nice too!).

So I Said to Myself ...

Have you ever watched someone talk to him- or herself? Amusing, isn't it? I once watched a man at a restaurant carry on an entire conversation with himself over a waffle. He could hardly take a bite, he was so mad at whoever it was he was telling off.

While most of us don't converse with ourselves aloud like that, many of us talk to ourselves silently. Sometimes, it's not all that encouraging.

"Why'd you do that?"

"How could you be so stupid?"

"You're such a loser!"

"Nobody likes you."

And so on. And so on. And so on. In fact, some of the worst criticism we'll ever hear in our lives will come from our own inner voice. That inner voice can give us scathing reviews right in the midst of positive input from others. And to which voice do you think we usually listen? The negative one. To which voice should we listen? The positive one, of course.

Does this scene sound familiar?

"You did a great job in the play," someone will say to you.

"Is he crazy?" you think. "I was horrible!"

Or your best friend will tell you, "That new haircut really looks cute on you," and your inner voice will answer, "Is she blind? It looks terrible! I hate it! I'm not coming out of my house until the next millennium."

These negative appraisals aren't coming from God. God is

an encourager. His voice says things like:

"You may have failed this time, but I still believe in you."

"You might feel like a loser right now, but you're a winner with me."

"It may seem like you have no friends today, but don't ever forget that I gave my life for you."

Look at how God responded to Peter after he denied him. Did he tell Peter, "You are such a wimp in the face of danger. Why didn't you stand up for me? After all I've done for you, the least you could have done was say you knew me, but you couldn't even do that. Thanks a lot. What kind of friend are you anyway?"

Jesus didn't say anything like that, though. Peter had failed him. Three times in one day, to be exact. Yet Jesus didn't reinforce Peter's failure with words of discouragement. He forgave him, he encouraged him, and most importantly, he still used him.

Do you know, too, that when Jesus commanded us to love our neighbor, he gave the example that we're to love him or her as we love ourselves? That means God expects us to be kind to ourselves, to nourish and care for our bodies and minds, and to encourage ourselves with our own words.

So be careful of your internal conversations. Tell yourself positive things, and listen for the encouraging messages from God. He'll speak them through his Word, in that still small voice in your heart, and through the encouragement of others. God is talking, but you have to tune out all of that other stuff to hear him.

Thoughts to Ponder

Do you think you spend more time internally criticizing or encouraging yourself?

If Jesus could forgive Peter for his triple denial, what do you think that says about his understanding and mercy?

Bumper Sticker for the Day
Encouragement—sometimes it's an inside job.

Scripture to Stand On

If you really keep the royal law found in Scripture, "Love your neighbor as yourself," you are doing right.

JAMES 2:8

Hello Again, Lord ...

Lord, help me to remember to love, nurture, and respect myself enough, so that when I love my neighbor as myself, it means something.

You Said a Mouthful

One of the most destructive forces known to man isn't a smart bomb, a Daisy Cutter, or even my cooking. It's the tongue. The tongue has been responsible for a lot of destruction, injury, devastation, misunderstanding, wars, and other calamities through the centuries.

No wonder there are so many scriptures in James that deal with the tongue. "The tongue is a fire," "an unruly evil, full of deadly poison," "a world of iniquity," "no man can tame it."

Not only is the tongue capable of plenty of mayhem, the Bible says it's a gauge of our spirituality, too.

God tells us here in James that we can go to church every Sunday, empty our pockets into the offering plate, help out with children's church, and do all sorts of public acts of apparent holiness, but if we tell half-truths, bear false witness against others, speak discouragement, and allow our tongues to be used for evil, then our religion is in vain. It means zippo. Nada. It's useless to us and to God. All the good we do means nothing if our tongue is out of order.

The tongue and the words it utters are important to God. Not because he needs to use them to gauge the condition of our hearts, but because we do. God already knows what we have harbored in our hearts. He wants us to realize it, too, by paying closer attention to our words.

A truly holy heart won't speak half-truths. A truly holy heart won't spread inuendo about others behind their backs. A truly

16

holy heart won't plan evil against someone else. A truly holy heart will have a truly loving tongue.

It's as simple as that.

Thoughts to Ponder

Think about some of the words you've been using lately. What do they say about your heart?

Why do you think your words reveal what's going on inside of you?

Bumper Sticker for the Day
Your tongue can be an instrument of peace or a weapon of mass destruction.

Scripture to Stand On

The tongue also is a fire, a world of evil among the parts of the body. It corrupts the whole person, sets the whole course of his life on fire, and is itself set on fire by hell.

JAMES 3:6

Hello Again, Lord ...

Lord, help me to keep you in my heart, and my tongue out of trouble.

Guess Who

Have you ever tried to solve one of those puzzles where they've made a single face out of several different celebrities? It might be Brad Pitt's nose, Bruce Willis' ears, Ray Romano's chin, and so on. The finished product barely looks human, and it's your job to figure out which facial part belongs to which celebrity.

Sometimes that's what we try doing with our own identities. We're a little bit of this person, and a little more of that person over there. We add a dash of him, and a scoop of her, and by the time we're finished, there's very little of us left in the picture.

When God created us, he designed us to be unique individuals, not clones of someone else. He didn't want us to look, act, think, sing, draw, write, play an instrument, or do anything exactly like someone else. We each have our own distinct personalities, which may not even be fully developed yet. We each have our own set of memories that have helped form who we are. We each have our own desires, goals, and dreams. We each have our own gifts. We each have our own talents. We each have our own passion. We each have our own vision. We each have our own life. God has a custom-designed plan for each one of us, but it's up to us to follow it.

God wants us to walk through the doors he opens to us. He wants us to persevere through the discouragements. He wants us to let him lead. He doesn't want us doing anything that will sidetrack us from his perfect will. He doesn't want to share our attention. He doesn't want to share our allegiance. He doesn't want to share the credit when good things happen to us. He loves us and doesn't want us settling for anything less than his best. God knows exactly who we are and what we can accomplish with his help.

Do we?

Thoughts to Ponder

Why do you think God wants you to fulfill his plan for your life?

Knowing that God has a lot invested in you, how does it make you feel?

Bumper Sticker for the Day
Sometimes we're pushing on the door we want God to open, while his sign says "Pull."

Scripture to Stand On

But if you harbor bitter envy and selfish ambition in your hearts, do not boast about it or deny the truth.

JAMES 3:14

Hello Again, Lord ...

Lord, I give you control of my life. Lead me in the paths that you want me to go.

Name Tags

Chances are, you have been to a party where the host or hostess distributed name tags to the guests so everyone could communicate better with each other. This makes it so much easier than saying, "Hey, You In The Red Dress, you're standing on my foot," or "Guy In The Fish Tie, could you please pass the chips?" Name tags help us know who it is we're talking to.

If God wore a name tag, what do you suppose his name tag would say?

"God the Father."

"God the Provider."

"God the Comforter."

"God the Healer."

"God the Omnipotent One."

There are plenty of names that could be written on God's name tag, aren't there?

Do you realize, too, that if you were handed someone else's name tag, and you accidentally put it on and wore it, it might cause some confusion, but it wouldn't change your identity one bit? Of course, you know that. You're still who you are, no matter what name tag you happen to be wearing.

If someone were to put a different name tag on God, it wouldn't change his identity either. If they were to call him "Unloving," "Unconcerned," or even "Nonexistent," it wouldn't change a single thing about who he truly is. Just as we are who we are in spite of the name tag someone has incorrectly placed on us, God is who he is regardless of the incorrect labels people try to put on him.

The Bible gives us a lot of insight into God's characteristics. It describes his qualities for us in perfect detail. So, no matter what name tag someone places on him, we can always go to God's Word and discover for ourselves what kind of God he really is.

Name tags—when you're at a party, make sure they give you the right one. And when someone places a name tag on God, make sure his or her information is correct, too.

Thoughts to Ponder

Describe who God is to you.

Read some of the descriptions of God that are in the Bible. Do these descriptions match the God that you know?

Bumper Sticker for the Day
God knows everything about you.
What do you know about him?

Scripture to Stand On

Every good and perfect gift is from above, coming down from the Father of the heavenly lights, who does not change like shifting shadows.

JAMES 1:17

Hello Again, Lord ...

Lord, thank you for being the God you are. Help me to spend more time getting to know you better.

Gnats, Gopherwood, and Grace

Do you overlook your own faults while putting other people's faults under a microscope? It's easy to do. Jesus even talked about this kind of human behavior when he told the Pharisees, "You strain out a gnat, but swallow a camel." In other words, they were fretting over everyone else's minor infractions of the law, while ignoring their own major ones.

Jesus said something similar to his disciples and the people gathered to hear him speak one day. He said, "First take the plank out of your eye, and then you will see clearly to remove the speck from your brother's eye." Again, loosely translated, it means, "clean up that pile of debris you've shoved under your own bed before you criticize the pencil that rolled under your brother's or sister's."

If each one of us spent the necessary time scrutinizing our own actions, we wouldn't have so much free time to scrutinize the behavior of others. That's the point that Jesus was making in both of these instances. He made the same point when the woman who was caught in adultery was brought to him. The crowd, wanting him to condemn her for her sin, found him condemning their sins as well. "You who are without sin cast the first stone."

No one could cast that first stone because each one of them was guilty of something. Jesus made them take a good hard look inside themselves, and their self-righteousness couldn't stand.

Jesus sees through our facade, that act we put on for others and even for ourselves. He looks straight into our hearts. Imagine how foolish we must look to him, standing there with countless banners draped across our chest that say, "pride," "envy," "jealousy," "gossip," "unkindness," "intolerance," while we piously condemn someone else for whatever their banner happens to say.

When it comes to other people's faults, we must look at them as we would want Christ to look at our faults—through the eyes of grace.

Thoughts to Ponder

To whom do you tend to grant more grace—yourself or others?

If Jesus talked this much about our tendencies to judge others more harshly than we judge ourselves, do you think he was serious about it?

Bumper Sticker for the Day
It's amazing how much our eyesight improves when we look inward first.

Scripture to Stand On

Wash your hands, you sinners, and purify your hearts, you double-minded.

JAMES 4:8b

Hello Again, Lord ...

Lord, help me to examine my own heart before recommending surgery on someone else's.

Been There, Made It Through That

We don't have to look very far in the Bible to find examples of patience in the face of suffering.

Joseph had to deal with the jealousy of his brothers, and once he was away from them, he was even falsely accused of rape by the wife of his boss, and thrown into prison. Yet God was faithful, and he was eventually made second in command over all of Egypt and ended up being instrumental in saving his own family from starvation.

Job had to deal with tremendous loss. Yet God was faithful and restored everything he had lost, and then some.

Noah was ridiculed for following God's will. Yet God was faithful and saved Noah and his family from the Great Flood.

And then there was David. He had to deal with the jealousy of Saul. Yet God was faithful and David eventually took his rightful place as king.

So why do you think God wanted to tell us their stories? Maybe he wanted to make sure we knew that when we're faced with tough situations, we're not alone. Maybe he wanted us to tell ourselves, "If Joseph could deal with his brothers selling him into slavery, then I can deal with mine wearing my new jacket without asking." Or, "If Noah could put up with the ridicule he faced, I can put up with a few stares in the cafeteria when I bow my head to say grace."

The Bible gives us plenty more examples of men and women who not only handled their difficult circumstances in a trusting and patient way, but had their faith actually grow from the experience. If you need encouragement right now for something you're going through, read the story of one of these prophets of God. It'll encourage you. It'll help you persevere. And it'll probably make what you're facing seem pretty minor by comparison.

Thoughts to Ponder

Are you going through a difficult time right now?

Is there a person in the Bible who faced circumstances similar to what you're going through? How did he or she handle it?

Bumper Sticker for the Day
The easiest way to stay on the right path is to walk in the footsteps of those who have gone that way before.

Scripture to Stand On

Brothers, as an example of patience in the face of suffering, take the prophets who spoke in the name of the Lord.

JAMES 5:10

Hello Again, Lord ...

Lord, thank you for your Word. It always says just the right thing.

Tongue Depressor

Do you ever find yourself in a situation where you're about to tell someone something, but you're not sure whether or not it's gossip? Since you're not sure, you quickly preface it with, "OK, I'll tell you, but don't tell anyone that you heard it from me." (Just for the record, if you're afraid of being quoted, it's probably gossip.)

But if you still can't decide whether something you're about to say is coming from gossip or love, here are some more helpful ways to tell the difference:

Gossip hurts.	Love heals.
Gossip hinders.	Love helps.
Gossip believes the worst.	Love hopes for the best.
Gossip hates truth.	Love hates innuendo.
Gossip edits the positive.	Love hears only the positive.
Gossip reacts without the facts.	Love doesn't change even if it's true.
Gossip discourages.	Love uplifts.
Gossip takes it to others.	Love takes it to God.
Gossip adds to the story.	Love verifies the story.
Gossip reveals hidden jealousies.	Love proves its loyalty.
Gossip accuses.	Love defends.
Gossip destroys.	Love builds.
Gossip is usually whispered.	Love isn't ashamed.
Gossip manipulates facts.	Love sticks to the facts.

Gossip doesn't want to be quoted.	Love would write it down and sign it.
Gossip is sneaky.	Love is bold.
Gossip feeds on the failings of people.	Love brings out the best in people.
Gossip loses friends.	Love keeps them.
Gossip is hard to stop.	Love is impossible to stop.

Thoughts to Ponder

When someone shares some gossip with you, do you usually ...
a. listen, then pass it on?
b. listen, but keep it to yourself?
c. look for creative ways you can leak the gossip—for example, "prayer requests," "accidentally" slipping the gossip into a conversation, etc.
d. defend the person being gossiped about?

How would you want your friends to respond to any gossip they might hear about you?

Bumper Sticker for the Day
Gossip—one language you don't want to learn.

Scripture to Stand On

If anyone considers himself religious and yet does not keep a tight rein on his tongue, he deceives himself and his religion is worthless.

JAMES 1:26

Hello Again, Lord ...

Lord, help me to remember that my tongue needs its rest, too.

Who Wants to Be a Gazillionaire?

Winning millions of dollars may sound nice on the surface, but having endless amounts of money comes at a price, too. Not that I know firsthand, but I've heard that whenever someone comes into a lot of money, all of a sudden that person finds him- or herself with scores of friends. Often these are people who never gave that person the time of day before. All of a sudden every organization and investment firm is calling him or her with surefire ways to invest the money. All of a sudden the millionaire is hearing from relatives he or she didn't even know existed. Money didn't solve this person's problems. It just created a whole new set of them.

Don't get me wrong. Money is nice. A full wallet is much more fun than one with only dust inside. Yet James warns us of the danger of putting riches before God. He reminds us that gold and silver (and savings accounts, new cars, CDs, and the latest fashions) are all temporary. They have absolutely no eternal value. They'll be like that cool new shirt we couldn't live without six years ago that we wouldn't be caught dead in today. That's how earthly riches are going to appear to us in eternity.

"I can't believe he wasted all his time on that."

"She loved that more than God? Puh-lllease. Can we say shallow?"

It's fine to work hard and make money, but money shouldn't be at the center of our lives. Money shouldn't determine our happiness. We need to be content, whether we have a lot or a little. Money shouldn't be our hope. The rich get sick and suffer losses, too. Money shouldn't be our path to popularity. The friends who love us because of our possessions will be the first to leave when we no longer have them.

Money. It's going to be out of fashion in eternity.

Thoughts to Ponder

If you could choose between having unlimited riches but being miserable and alone, or simply having all your needs met and being happy, which would be your choice?

What do you think are some of the dangers of putting the pursuit of money before God?

Bumper Sticker for the Day
At the pearly gates, there is no cash line.

Scripture to Stand On

Your gold and silver are corroded. Their corrosion will testify against you and eat your flesh like fire. You have hoarded wealth in the last days.

JAMES 5:3

Hello Again, Lord ...

Lord, help me to appreciate how you've always met my needs, to work hard for the things I want, and to never forget what's truly important in life.

The Problem

OK, here's the problem ... no one ever lets me know what's going on in youth group."

"OK, here's the problem ... no one seems to care when I miss a meeting."

"OK, here's the problem ... I'd love to be on the youth drama team, but no one's ever asked me."

"OK, here's the problem ... we always sing the same songs during praise and worship. Can't we sing something new?"

"OK, here's the problem ... I don't know why I've got to sit here at this bake sale table after church. No one ever stops by. What's wrong with my brownies anyway?"

"OK, here's the problem ... why do I always get stuck washing the cars at these youth car washes while everyone else gets to just stand on the corner waving at people?"

"OK, here's the problem ... how come there are never any refreshments at youth group?"

"OK, here's the problem ..."

Analyzing "the problem" is the easy part. Anyone can do that. You just sit back and make a mental list of everything you wish would improve. Yet if you truly want things to get better, as opposed to wanting only to point out flaws, you'll take some action. Volunteer to be a part of the solution:

"I'll volunteer to make calls to everyone and let them know about our upcoming youth events."

"Maybe we should have our own newsletter. I can help with that."

"I'll send a 'We missed you' card to everyone who wasn't at our last meeting."

"I'll let the drama leader know I'm interested in acting. He'll never know I like to act unless I tell him."

"I'll tell our youth pastor about this great song I heard. I think I could even teach it to the group if he'd like me to."

"Maybe people don't know we're having a bake sale. I think I'll make some signs, and I could have some music playing. Maybe I'll make up some flyers, too."

"The car wash is this Saturday. Maybe I'll suggest to the youth pastor that we make up a schedule, so we'll be able to take turns washing the cars and waving the people in."

"I think I'll volunteer to bring refreshments to our next youth meeting." (I personally would never do this because of the medical liability involved with my cooking, but your brownies might not glow like mine do.)

The bottom line is that anyone can complain. But solving a problem takes more than that. It takes someone who's more action than words.

Thoughts to Ponder

Name some things about your youth group that you feel might need improving.

In what ways can you help in these areas?

Bumper Sticker for the Day
Complaints are heard best when accompanied by an offer to help.

Scripture to Stand On

But someone will say, "You have faith; I have deeds." Show me your faith without deeds, and I will show you my faith by what I do.

JAMES 2:18

Hello Again, Lord ...

Lord, help me not to just point out problems, but to be a part of the solution.

Harmless Words?

Think that negative little comment you made about someone at lunch today with your friends was harmless?

Think again.

Gossip hurts. It discourages. It destroys relationships. It kills
trust. And not only can it hurt the subject of the gossip, it can
hurt the gossiper, too.

How's that?

Well, when people gossip, they don't realize how far their
words can travel. Sure, they know the gossip will make its way
to the people they want it to reach (after all, isn't that why
people gossip in the first place? To get misinformation out to
as many people as possible?).

Yet gossip almost always travels a little farther than that.
Gossip has a way of finding its way back to the person being
gossiped about. That person may never confront the gossiper
over it, but rest assured, he or she has heard every word the
gossiper said.

If he or she has the courage to confront the gossiper, it's
interesting to watch how quickly the backpeddling starts.

"Oh, that's not at all what I meant by that," they'll say, as the
beads of sweat begin to form on their foreheads. They'll make
up excuses, say they were misquoted, blame others, and even
try to blame the gossip on the victim. "You misunderstood,"
they'll say, eyeing the quickest exit.

Maybe the first step toward ending gossip is to admit our
own involvement in it. Yes, gossip hurts. Gossip discourages.

Gossip destroys relationships. Gossip kills trust. It's far from harmless. And most importantly, God hates it.

Thoughts to Ponder

Have you ever had to confront a gossiper over something he or she said?

How would it make you feel to find out that something you said about someone made it back to that person?

Bumper Sticker for the Day
If the tongue's a fire, who needs salsa?

Scripture to Stand On

If anyone is never at fault in what he says, he is a perfect man, able to keep his whole body in check.

JAMES 3:2b

Hello Again, Lord ...

Lord, help me to examine my words before they exit my mouth.

What Matters Most

God doesn't care about the size of your savings account, but he is interested in how much good you do with what you have.

God doesn't care whether or not you're wearing the hottest new shoes, but he does care where you walk in them.

The size of your house doesn't matter to God, but the size of your heart does.

Your grade point average, the college you get accepted into, or even your major doesn't impress God as much as how you treat others.

God doesn't care about the kind of car your family drives, as much as he cares about how many people you've brought to church in it.

God isn't interested in the value of the jewelry you wear, the stocks your family owns, or the rarity of your baseball card collection, but he is interested in whether you're making any investments in heaven.

Your popularity doesn't matter to God, but he is interested in whether you've told your friends about him.

How well you're connected doesn't matter as much to God as how well you're grounded.

God doesn't care if you can quote the law, but he is concerned with how much mercy you show others.

The frequency with which you go to church doesn't matter as much to God as the openness of your heart while you're there.

The size of your offering doesn't impress him as much as

IF THE TONGUE'S A FIRE, WHO NEEDS SALSA?

how much of yourself accompanies it.

God isn't as concerned with how boldly you speak for him as he is with how boldly you live for him.

Thoughts to Ponder

Do you think you've been more concerned with eternal things, or things that will pass?

In what ways do you think you can become more focused on eternal things?

Bumper Sticker for the Day
**Eternity—the only investment guaranteed
to never lose its value.**

Scripture to Stand On

Listen, my dear brothers: Has not God chosen those who are poor in the eyes of the world to be rich in faith and to inherit the kingdom he promised those who love him?

JAMES 2:5

Hello Again, Lord ...

Lord, instead of focusing my attention on what I have here and now, help me to see the importance of what I'm doing for eternity.

A Sweeping Victory

Do you hate sweeping your floor? Sure, it's nice to walk on after it's done, but the process can be a pain, can't it? You might even be tempted to take a shortcut and sweep all those dust balls, wads of paper, broken pens, chewed-up pencils, paper clips, and whatever else has taken up residence on your floor, under the rug so no one will see it. Yet rugs aren't supposed to look like a relief map of the Smoky Mountains. They're supposed to be flat. Sweeping all that mess under the rug doesn't get rid of any of it. It just makes it look more presentable. But you know it's there. God knows it's there. And your mom probably has a pretty good idea that it's there, too.

Sometimes we are tempted to take a few shortcuts in cleaning up the messes in our lives, too. Instead of putting envy, jealousy, greed, lust, hatred, and pride where they belong—under the grace of God—we try to hang on to them and tuck them away in our hearts, thinking no one will see them. We don't get rid of them, we just hide them. We may end up looking presentable to others, but God knows they're still there. And so do we.

Maybe it's time we all did a little spring cleaning in our hearts, to see what we've got hidden in there. While we're at it, we may want to sweep out our rooms a little, too. But this time, try not to sweep anything under the rug ... unless you've got dependable mountain-climbing equipment.

Thoughts to Ponder

Why do you think it's important to search your heart for anything that might be displeasing to God?

Is there a behavior, attitude, or habit in your life that you've been trying to pretend isn't there?

Bumper Sticker for the Day
When God washes your heart, all the corners get clean.

Scripture to Stand On

Therefore, get rid of all moral filth and the evil that is so prevalent ...
JAMES 1:21a

Hello Again, Lord ...

Lord, help me to trust you with my heart—even those areas I've tried to hide from you.

If There's Anything I Can Do ...

I wrote a comedy sketch once for church drama groups called "If There's Anything We Can Do." It's in my book *Reality Check* (Lillenas Publishing Company). It's about a church visitation committee who visit a lady whose husband has just passed away. The members of the visitation committee keep asking the lady if there's anything they can do to help, but every time the lady suggests something, they have an excuse as to why they can't meet that particular request. Then they quickly follow it up with yet another, "But if there's anything else we can do ..."

Sounds like a lot of us, doesn't it? We want to help those around us, but we want to help them at the time and in the way we want, not necessarily in the way and at the time they need help.

We want to say, "If you need anything, don't hesitate to call," while all the time keeping a close hand on our wallet. We want to sign a card with the word "love" right above our name, but we don't want to have to do anything to show real love. We want to ask people about their relationships with God, but never invite them to actually go to church with us. We want to do all the things that make our conscience feel better, that make us look very Christian, without having to really do anything significant to help.

When Jesus told Zaccheus, the unpopular tax collector, that he was going to go to his house for dinner, he went. When Mary and Martha came to him about their brother Lazarus, Jesus went and raised him from the dead. When the children sat on Jesus' lap and Jesus spent time with them, it wasn't simply a photo op. This was who Jesus was. He didn't just talk about loving others; he demonstrated it by his actions.

So, the next time you catch yourself telling someone, "If there's anything I can do," make sure you mean it. People need real love, the kind that's more than just a word on a card.

Thoughts to Ponder

When you hear of someone who has a true need, do you tend to offer that person real help, or mere lip service?

Why do you think it's important for you to follow through with your promises of help to people?

Bumper Sticker for the Day
All the words in the world won't fill a hungry stomach.

Scripture to Stand On

Suppose a brother or sister is without clothes and daily food. If one of you says to him, "Go, I wish you well; keep warm and well fed," but does nothing about his physical needs, what good is it? In the same way, faith by itself, if it is not accompanied by action, is dead.

JAMES 2:15-17

Hello Again, Lord ...

Lord, when people need a hand, help me not to wave "bye" with mine.

Within the Ranks

We're pretty good at telling others about God—most of the time. We know the good news and we're ready to share it with those who haven't heard yet.

But when it comes to fellow Christians who stumble, we're not as eager to tell them about God's mercy and love. After all, how dare they fall? How dare they make a mistake in judgment? How dare they turn from the straight and narrow?

Here in James, though, we're being told how we're supposed to handle those around us who wander from the truth. We're supposed to help bring them back. We're supposed to show them forgiveness, just as we've been shown mercy and forgiveness for our wrongdoings. We're supposed to encourage them and "cover a multitude of sins."

Unfortunately, we don't do a lot of covering, do we? We don't want to cover even one of their sins, much less a multitude.

"Have you heard? Neil got involved with drugs."

"Can you believe it? I just heard the news about Sheri and Jeff. I always knew she was, well, you know ..."

Another comedy sketch that I wrote is called "The Gossip Gazette." It's about a group of people who put out a weekly paper called "The Gossip Gazette" that tells all the latest news of the church. Only it's not the same news that usually gets written up in the church bulletin. This is the news you hear about only in the restaurant after church, or on the telephone the following week.

When one of our fellow believers wanders, our hearts should ache for him or her. Why? Because God's does. We should see the good that's still left in that person. Why? Because God does. We should lift that person up, instead of tearing him or her down. Why? Because God does.

If our love is real, we'll do everything we can to get fellow believers back on track. Why? Because that's what God does, and we're supposed to do it, too. Yet, if our discouraging words keep them heading in the wrong direction, then we've failed God. Maybe even more than they have.

Thoughts to Ponder

When you hear of a fellow believer who has stumbled, what is your first reaction? Is it one of judgment or one of mercy?

When you make a mistake, how do you want people to treat you? With judgment or with mercy?

Bumper Sticker for the Day
It's hard to lift others up when we're stepping on their toes.

Scripture to Stand On

My brothers, if one of you should wander from the truth and someone should bring him back, remember this: Whoever turns a sinner from the error of his way will save him from death and cover over a multitude of sins.

JAMES 5:19

Hello Again, Lord ...

Lord, help me to remember that even believers need love and mercy, too.

Who's the Boss?

When a mother is always overriding what the father is saying, or vice versa, it makes it very difficult for the children, doesn't it?

"Mom, can I go bowling Friday night?"

"What'd your father say?"

"He said no."

"Then go on. Have a good time. But don't be out late."

It's just as confusing when an employee goes over a supervisor's head, a student goes over a teacher's head, and so on. People are placed in authority for a reason. It's important to know who the authorities are in each of life's situations and to treat those people accordingly.

When we don't know, don't accept, or don't honor the instructions of the authority figures in our life, or when authority figures undermine each other, confusion results. We don't know whether to listen to our mother and go bowling or listen to our father and stay home. We don't know if we should listen to our teacher when he says we need to study for a test on Friday, or listen to our friend who says, "How hard can it be? Let's go to the arcade instead."

Conflicting instructions sometimes even occur among Christians. This one says it's wrong to do this. That one says it's wrong to do that. How do we know who's right?

The Bible tells us that God is the ultimate authority figure in life. So before you take someone's word for anything, go to the ultimate authority's guidebook for life. See what he says in his Word. He's the boss. His Word is the final word.

Thoughts to Ponder

Why do you think God wants you to submit yourself to his will?

Who would you say has been in charge of your life lately?

Bumper Sticker for the Day
If God's not the boss of your life, give him a promotion.

Scripture to Stand On

Submit yourselves, then, to God.

JAMES 4:7a

Hello Again, Lord ...

Help me to remember that you, Lord, are the CEO of life.

For Example

Have you ever met people who claimed to be Christians but did very little to back it up? They weren't kind to others. They were selfish. They had prejudices. They were trouble-makers. They weren't patient. They weren't considerate of other people's feelings. They gossiped. They bullied. They were prideful. They were discouragers. They envied others. And so on and so on and so on.

There are certain characteristics that unbelievers expect a believer to have. It's pretty basic. They're the characteristics of Christ. See, people know how Jesus acted. They know what he would and wouldn't have done in certain circumstances. When we don't exhibit those same characteristics, it confuses them. They wonder about the validity of what we say.

Think about your own behavior. If an unbeliever at your school, at your workplace, or maybe even within your family had to fill out a questionnaire about you, how would he or she answer the following questions?

Would you say he/she is a self-sacrificing person?
Would you say he/she is humble?
Would you say he/she is patient?
Would you say he/she is kind?
Would you say he/she spreads gossip?
Would you say he/she is prideful?
Would you say he/she is selfish?
Would you say he/she is envious?

Would you say he/she is longsuffering?
Would you say he/she always sees the best in a person?
Would you say he/she truly loves others?

What do you think those around you would say about your walk of faith? If the answers aren't very good, that could be one reason why they're still unbelievers.

Thoughts to Ponder

In what ways do you think you need to change to be a better example of Christ?

Do you think it's important for believers to walk the talk in their attitudes and actions?

Bumper Sticker for the Day
Faith—if it's not real, it won't appeal.

Scripture to Stand On

What good is it, my brothers, if a man claims to have faith but has no deeds? Can such faith save him?

JAMES 2:14

Hello Again, Lord ...

Lord, help me to act in a way that will line up with what I say.

Prayer Lite

Before we pray, are there any needs that you'd like us to remember?"

"Yes, please pray for my brother. His cancer has returned."

"Pray for my friend. He was seriously hurt in a car wreck."

"Pray that I'll be able to find the right shoes to go with my new dress for the concert."

"Pray for my Dad to find work. He's been out of a job for three months now."

"Pray for my mom to recover from her knee surgery."

"Pray for my little brother to quit poking me in the arm every time I'm trying to watch TV."

Somehow buying a new pair of shoes and having a bothersome brother seem to pale in comparison to cancer or a serious injury, don't they?

And while your little brother's habit of poking your arm can be quite annoying, it's really nothing compared to long-term unemployment or surgery.

Sometimes we pray about some pretty shallow things, don't we?

Does this mean, though, that God can't answer our prayers about small problems, too? Of course not. God is interested in every aspect of our lives. Yet we need to recognize the difference between serious needs and everyday needs. Otherwise, we become very shallow people.

Finding the right shoes to go with a dress is not a serious matter. God can help us find them, but if we're so busy shopping that we don't think twice about our friend whose brother is battling cancer, we're being pretty self-focused.

That may sound obvious to most of us, but believe it or not, some people think their fashion problems and someone else's life-threatening illness are somehow equal. They're not.

Life gives some of us some pretty serious challenges. If you have nothing serious going on in your life at the moment, count your blessings. But don't try to raise the urgency of your dilemma to that of truly serious matters. Know the difference. Thank God that your brother isn't battling cancer. Thank God that your parent or parents have jobs, no matter what they're getting paid. Thank God that your friend wasn't seriously injured in a car wreck. Thank God for your blessings, and remember to pray for the challenges of those around you.

If your little brother still won't quit poking you in the arm, tell your mom or dad, or get up and move to another room. When you're ready to look at your problem from a different perspective, you might even find yourself thanking God that your brother is healthy enough to bug you.

Thoughts to Ponder

When is the last time you prayed for someone else's need?

Make a list of some of your many blessings.

Bumper Sticker for the Day
**Ever wonder why no one ever said
"Long Live the Drama Queen"?**

Scripture to Stand On

Is any one of you sick? He should call the elders of the church to pray over him and anoint him with oil in the name of the Lord.

JAMES 5:14

Hello Again, Lord ...

Lord, help me not to get so caught up in the little challenges of life that I overlook the big ones.

Go Away

Have you ever had to ignore someone, hoping that he or she would eventually go away? Maybe you weren't sure of your safety with this individual. Maybe you weren't sure what he or she wanted, but something about this person made you feel uneasy.

"Look, just give me your phone number and I'll leave you alone," this person pleads.

Of course, you don't do it. If you want someone to leave you alone, giving that person your phone number would be the last thing you'd want to do.

"OK, then, just tell me your address."

No, again. Why would you give your address to someone who you want to leave you alone?

"All right, let's keep it impersonal. Just give me your email address. That's all I want. Just your email address and you'll never hear from me again."

Well, first of all, why would he or she need your email address if you were never going to hear from him or her? Second, if you don't want someone bothering you, why would you give him or her a means to contact you? It's just common sense that if you want someone to go away, you ignore him or her.

The Bible says that's how we're to handle the enemy. We're to resist him. If we do, if we resist what he's saying, if we don't listen to his lies, he will flee from us. It doesn't say he'll go off and sulk. It says that he'll flee. To flee means to run away swiftly, to vanish.

So the next time you're tempted to do something you shouldn't do, follow God's advice and resist the tempter. Don't give him any of your time, your attention, or your reputation. Ignore him, then sit back and watch him flee.

Thoughts to Ponder

Why do you think you shouldn't give the enemy any of your time or attention?

When you're tempted to do something you shouldn't, what can you do to help yourself resist?

Bumper Sticker for the Day
When the enemy knocks, don't put out the welcome mat.

Scripture to Stand On

Resist the devil, and he will flee from you.

JAMES 4:7b

Hello Again, Lord ...

Lord, help me to remember that if I keep my mind on you, it won't go where it shouldn't.

Goin' the Distance

A friend of mine recently passed away. She was ninety-nine and a half years old. Did she have an easy life? No. As a matter of fact, she had a pretty tough one. Yet she persevered in spite of her circumstances. Even though she had her own health problems, she outlived her pastor/husband, a daughter, and countless other relatives and friends. How did she do it? She was blessed by God, of course, but also she didn't give up.

Picture yourself sitting at a bus stop, waiting for your bus to come. You've been there for hours and finally decide to give up on it and walk away. Just as you turn the corner, though, the bus comes, and you miss it. Would it matter how many hours you had waited for that bus if you weren't there when it eventually came?

We don't get into trouble when we think the bus is late. After all, we've waited this long for the bus, what's another hour or two? We get into trouble when we somehow convince ourselves that the bus isn't coming at all.

"Something must have happened."

"Maybe there was a change in routing."

"They must have cancelled this bus."

When we start thinking it's not coming at all, that's when we feel justified in walking away. We give up on it, we fail to persevere, and we miss out.

Perseverance is a quality necessary for success. Think about it—without perseverance that one-hundred-yard dash would be the fifty-five-yard dash. Football teams would play for only three quarters and call it a night. Your favorite movie would never have been made, your favorite book would never have been written, and your favorite song would stop at a verse and half a chorus.

Every single person who has ever accomplished anything in life has had to persevere. Some have had to persevere through some pretty difficult circumstances. Yet they did it.

And you can, too.

Thoughts to Ponder

Would you say that you tend to persevere or give up too soon?

Think of something that you've accomplished that never would have happened had you not persevered.

Bumper Sticker for the Day
Be like a Velcro salesman and stick to your work.

Scripture to Stand On

You have heard of Job's perseverance and have seen what the Lord finally brought about.

JAMES 5:11b

Hello Again, Lord ...

Lord, don't let me give up when I should be looking up.

You What?!

Do you realize that when someone asks if he or she can confide in us, and we agree, we're not only promising to keep that person's confidence, but we're also assuring him or her that our friendship isn't going to change after hearing it?

When friends tell us what's on their hearts, it's because they're trusting us to still be their friends afterward. They don't expect, nor do they deserve, to receive a cold shoulder or unreturned telephone calls because now that we know the things they "struggle with," they're not really the kind of friend we want to have hanging around.

Don't get me wrong. There certainly are dangers in having negative influences in your life. Jesus warns us of that. But being a friend to someone preconfession and ignoring him or her postconfession, doesn't seem very Christian, does it? Jesus saw the sins of the woman at the well, yet he still was a friend to her. He also saw Mary Magdalene's sins, yet he still was a friend to her. He's our example. We're supposed to act like him.

If a friend opens up to you it's because there's something about you that makes him or her feel safe. Your friend feels you can be trusted with his or her faults. Don't prove your friend wrong by disappearing after he or she confesses them.

Thoughts to Ponder

How do you treat others' confidences?

How would you feel if you confided something in a friend and he or she treated you differently afterward?

Bumper Sticker for the Day
God's love is knowing the worst about someone, and still seeing only his or her best.

Scripture to Stand On

Brothers, do not slander one another. Anyone who speaks against his brother or judges him speaks against the law and judges it. When you judge the law, you are not keeping it, but sitting in judgment on it.

JAMES 4:11

Hello Again, Lord ...

Thank you, Lord, for being a friend that I can talk to about anything.

Can Do

Before you go anywhere today, I want you to clean your room."

"Uh-huh ..."

"And it wouldn't hurt to straighten your closet, too."

"Uh-huh ..."

"And do your laundry."

"Right."

"And take out the trash."

"Trash. Got it."

"And feed the dog."

"Will do.... So can I go now?"

"Go? Didn't you hear me? Not until your chores are done."

"All right.... So when are you going to tell me?"

"Tell you what?"

"What chores you want me to do."

We don't always pay attention to the things we're told, do we? Often instructions have a pretty short trip in one of our ears and out the other.

Unfortunately, that's how it is with God's instructions, too, sometimes. We read them in his Word, we hear them in sermon after sermon, Sunday school lesson after Sunday school lesson, but we don't act on them. We hear what we're supposed to be doing, but it doesn't sink in. It doesn't register. It doesn't seem important enough.

God tells us here in James that it is important. He says that we're to be doers of the Word, and not hearers only. God's

Word isn't supposed to just go in one ear and out the other. It's supposed to stay. It's supposed to become part of our lives. We're supposed to act on it. We're supposed to listen and then do what we're told. In other words, when God talks, we're supposed to pay attention.

Thoughts to Ponder

Think of three ways that you can become more of a doer of God's Word.

How different do you think the world would be if none of us were "doers" of God's Word?

Bumper Sticker for the Day
When you hear God's Word, act on what you've heard.

Scripture to Stand On

Do not merely listen to the word, and so deceive yourselves. Do what it says.

JAMES 1:22

Hello Again, Lord ...

Lord, your Word is more than nice sayings for wall plaques. It's my instructions for life.

Rain, Rain, Go Away

Imagine praying and asking God to stop the rain so your football game won't be cancelled, and having him stop it.

Imagine praying and asking him to make the sun come out so you can go surfing, and having him do it.

That's the kind of relationship Elijah had with God. Elijah asked God for big things. He didn't limit God. He had faith that God could do whatever he wanted to do. So asking him to stop the rain was no big deal. If it was in his will, Elijah knew that God would do it.

It must have been in God's will, too, because the Bible tells us that even though Elijah was a man just like us, when he prayed with all his heart and asked God to not let it rain for three and a half years, God didn't let it rain for three and a half years. Then, when Elijah prayed for the rain to return, the rain returned.

Can you imagine having that kind of faith? Elijah didn't use his faith for things like football games or surfing, though. When he prayed these requests, it was so that God's name would be glorified.

Sometimes we pray for things that have nothing whatsoever to do with God's name being glorified or God's will for our lives. We pray, and if God doesn't answer, we begin to question his love, his mercy, his purpose, and maybe even his power.

Yet God is a God who does love us. He is merciful, and he is all-powerful. So if he doesn't answer right away, maybe the problem isn't his failure to answer, but our failure to pray his will.

Thoughts to Ponder

Do you believe God is all-powerful?

Is there a situation in your life right now for which you're still waiting for God to answer?

Bumper Sticker for the Day
Prayer + God's will = our answer.

Scripture to Stand On

Elijah was a man just like us. He prayed earnestly that it would not rain, and it did not rain on the land for three and a half years.

JAMES 5:17

Hello Again, Lord ...

Lord, thank you for listening to all our prayers, even though you don't always say "yes."

Laying Down Your Tongue

I once knew a man who was always bragging about how he loved his friends so much that he would die for them. He figured that was the ultimate measure of love. Whether, if the occasion ever presented itself, he'd really do it was debatable. None of us truly know what we'd do in a situation like that. Most of our friendships can't even make it through the first misunderstanding, much less a sacrifice as great as death.

The funny thing about this man's claim was that he never said a kind word about any of these people that he would "die for." I often wanted to suggest, "Instead of laying down your life for your friends, why don't you just put your tongue to rest instead?"

Words are easy. We can say we love our friends enough to give our lives for them, but it means very little if we can't even give them the simple benefit of the doubt when misunderstandings occur. We can say we're praying for them, but how much more praying could we be doing if we weren't talking about them behind their backs?

The fact is, we don't really know what this "no greater love hath any man than to lay down his life for his friends" kind of love is all about. When we flippantly brag about how easily we would do it, we are, in a way, minimizing the remarkable sacrifice of Jesus.

What Jesus did wasn't an easy thing to do. He gave his life for the world in the midst of the world's rejection of him. He gave his life for a people who didn't care about how much he was sacrificing. He gave his life for his friends after they had turned their backs on him and after not one of them had stood up for him while he was being falsely accused. He gave his life for his friends and didn't even complain to his father about their ungratefulness or shortcomings. He simply said, "Father, forgive them for they know not what they do."

Love your friend so much that you'd give your life for him or her?

Love your enemies?

When you really think about it, Jesus did an incredible thing on that cross. And what he wants us to do is to be willing to sacrifice ourselves for others, too, but not in death, in life. In other words, he wants us to have a servant's heart to those around us, to show them mercy, and to love them both to their faces and behind their backs. If we can't handle these simple things, who cares whether or not we'd lay down our lives for anybody?

Thoughts to Ponder

Why do you think God cares more about how you treat others than about how you say you would treat them in a given circumstance?

What do you think of Jesus' sacrifice for us? Do you think it was an easy thing for him to do?

Bumper Sticker for the Day
True love can withstand the greatest tests.

Scripture to Stand On

Don't grumble against each other, brothers, or you will be judged. The Judge is standing at the door!

JAMES 5:9

Hello Again, Lord ...

Lord, help me to give myself to help others, and not just talk about it.

Ignored?

"I can't believe no one's passed me the salsa. I've got a bowl of chips here in front of me, and not one person has bothered to pass me the salsa. What—do they think I can't handle it? Do they think it's too spicy for me? I can handle spicy. I love spicy. So why don't they pass it to me? What am I supposed to do with a bunch of undipped chips? I can't eat undipped chips! It's unnatural. Look at them all ... just sitting there, dipping their chips, happy as you please. Don't they even care that I don't have any dip? All they're interested in is themselves. Well, that's just fine! Let 'em dip away! I hope that salsa melts the braces right off their teeth! It'll teach them a lesson about sharing!"

This may be a little exaggerated, but how many of us go through a similar debate in our heads when we want something? Yet, before we reprimand our friends for not passing the salsa, we need to reprimand ourselves for not asking for it.

In case you haven't noticed it yet, people aren't mindreaders. They don't know what you want unless you say so. Then, if they don't pass you the salsa, you can correctly think that their behavior is rude. But if you've never vocalized your desires, then you shouldn't really criticize others for not giving them to you.

Even God likes us to vocalize our requests. He's all-knowing, so he already is aware of our wants and desires, but he likes us to talk to him about them. In fact, James even says that the reason we don't have what we need is because we don't ask.

So the next time you find yourself sitting with a bowl of undipped chips, you need to speak up and say, "Could someone please pass me the salsa?"

And when you have a need, you need to speak up to God, too.

Thoughts to Ponder

Do you talk to God about your needs, or do you just sit and complain?

Why do you think God wants you to talk to him about your needs?

Bumper Sticker for the Day
God's ready to listen. Are you ready to talk?

Scripture to Stand On

You do not have, because you do not ask God.

JAMES 4:2b

Hello Again, Lord ...

Lord, help me to tell you my needs and trust you to meet them.

What a Concept!

"Do unto others as you would have them do unto you." We've heard that hundreds of times, haven't we? We may even have it hanging on the wall of our house or church. Yet what exactly does it mean?

It means:

If you don't like people talking about you behind your back, don't talk about other people behind their backs.

If you want to be forgiven for what you do wrong to others, forgive others for what they do wrong to you.

If you want to be given the benefit of the doubt, give others the benefit of the doubt.

If you want to be included in others' social plans, include others in your social plans.

If you want people to understand you, try to understand them.

If you want your friends to listen to you, listen to them.

If you want people to be considerate of your feelings, be considerate of other people's feelings.

If you want people to overlook your faults, overlook other people's faults.

If you don't want people holding a grudge against you, don't hold a grudge against them.

It's a rather simple concept, but it's important enough that Jesus summed up all the "laws" with these two—"Love the Lord your God with all your heart and with all your soul, and with all your strength, and with all your mind," and "Love your neighbor as yourself."

So simple. So life-changing. And so often overlooked.

Thoughts to Ponder

Would you say that you usually treat people the way you'd like them to treat you?

In what ways could you improve on how you treat others?

Bumper Sticker for the Day
**What you do comes back to you. So depending on what
you've done, you'll either be quite blessed someday,
or you'd better start to run!**

Scripture to Stand On

*Speak and act as those who are going to be judged by the law that gives
freedom.*

JAMES 2:12

Hello Again, Lord ...

Lord, before I act, help me to think about how my actions
would feel from the receiving end.

Late Pay

A lady, I don't even remember her name, still owes me twenty dollars for baby-sitting I did back when I was a teenager. I baby-sat her children for a week, but she never paid me. She kept putting me off until I finally gave up and just let it go.

Hmmm ... let's see ... how much would that be with interest?

When you do work for someone, you expect to get paid, don't you? Whether the arrangements are for five dollars an hour, six dollars an hour, a little more, or even less, you're counting on that money. You need it to pay your own bills, buy your own clothes, CDs, or whatever. It's money you have earned for honest labor.

You might not realize it, but the Bible even covers the subject of your paycheck. Talk about relevant. It says that when someone hires us to work, that person should honor his or her word and pay us.

The Bible is pretty amazing that way. Even though it was written thousands of years ago, it talks about a lot of things we deal with today. It has practical advice on how we should act at work, at play, in our relationships, and more. It's our handbook for life.

God is fair. He wants us to be fair with others, and for them to be fair to us, too. It's fair to be paid for the work you've done. It's fair to expect equal treatment and to give others equal treatment, no matter what their race, religion, or sex happens to be. If you're nice to people, it's fair to expect them to treat you nicely in return. It doesn't always work out that way, but it's fair to expect it.

Fairness—it's important to God.

As for my twenty dollars, I figure God has paid me for those hours of work in so many, many different ways. See, that's another thing about God. He's promised to take care of us every day of our lives. And he's always fair.

Thoughts to Ponder

How do you think God feels when you treat people unfairly?

Have you ever been treated unfairly? How did it make you feel?

Bumper Sticker for the Day
Games, and life, just go better when everyone plays fair.

Scripture to Stand On

Look! The wages you failed to pay the workmen who mowed your fields are crying out against you. The cries of the harvesters have reached the ears of the Lord Almighty.

JAMES 5:4

Hello Again, Lord ...

Lord, help me to always treat people as fairly as I want to be treated.

Oh, Yeah?

If you think about it, most arguments are rooted in want. People want respect. (And if they can't earn it, they'll demand it.)

People want pity. (Nobody knows the troubles they've seen ... or made up.)

People want what others have. (I'm so happy for them I could just cry. How come nothing good ever happens to me? They always get the breaks. Life just isn't fair!)

People want to keep what they have. ("I've worked hard to get what I have. Let them get their own.")

People want attention. ("I'll show them they can't push me around!")

People want to be a victim. ("I wish I could do that, but I can't afford to.... Work? Hmmm ... what's that?")

People want a scapegoat. ("It's all his fault. It's all her fault. I didn't do anything wrong.")

People want to win. ("Their success means I lose. I have to win any way I can.")

People want an audience. ("I'll throw this fit in front of people so they won't see my fears.")

People want control. ("Everyone has to answer to me for their choices.")

People want to bully. ("If I intimidate them, I'll always get my way.")

People want to hide. ("If I can be argumentative, no one will see my pain.")

People want to condemn. ("If I point out your failure, I will never have to face mine.")

People want to destroy. ("If I can destroy your reputation, mine will look better.")

People want to divert. ("Ignore what I'm doing wrong, but let me help you with what you're doing wrong.")

People want to argue. ("Oh, yeah?!")

For communication to work, both parties have to be equally open to listening to each other and to God. It can't be a matter of one side wanting everything their way and the other side giving in. That doesn't help anyone. For peace to last, both sides need to speak up and share their feelings. Then when a compromise is reached, both parties will feel good about it.

Thoughts to Ponder

Would you say you tend to be argumentative or a peacemaker?

Why do you think it's important to speak up for yourself, but to do it in a godly manner?

Bumper Sticker for the Day
Many love to fight, but few fight to love.

Scripture to Stand On

What causes fights and quarrels among you? Don't they come from your desires that battle within you?

JAMES 4:1

Hello Again, Lord ...

Lord, help me to know not only when to speak up, but how.

Neither Here Nor There

There's a place here in America called Four Corners. It's where four of our states—Arizona, New Mexico, Utah, and Colorado—all meet. You can stand at a certain spot and have one foot in New Mexico, one in Arizona, a hand in Utah, and your other hand in Colorado. A family of four can have each family member in a different state and still hug each other. You can eat a sandwich in New Mexico, then have dessert in Utah seconds later. You can call someone from Colorado, take one step and call him or her back from Arizona, then take another step and call from New Mexico. As you can see, Four Corners is a fun place to visit. It's fun to be in more than one place at the same time and to move between four different states that quickly.

When it comes to spiritual matters, we're supposed to be a lot more stable than that. We can't be for God in one place, like church, then take a few steps to another place, like school, and deny him. We can't be for everything he stands for on Sunday, then be against everything he stands for by Wednesday. God wants our faith to be consistent. He wants it to be something that he can count on, and that we can count on, too.

Know what you believe. If you don't know, read God's word and find out for yourself. Even if you have doubts, God can handle your doubts.

In other words, you might be able to have your feet and hands in four different states at the same time, but you can't have four different views of faith and be left standing on any true convictions.

Thoughts to Ponder

Do you know what you believe?

Why do you think you should have faith that doesn't change hourly?

Bumper Sticker for the Day
Ever-changing faith results in never-changing people.

Scripture to Stand On

You adulterous people, don't you know that friendship with the world is hatred toward God? Anyone who chooses to be a friend of the world becomes an enemy of God.

JAMES 4:4

Hello Again, Lord ...

Thank you that you are a God who can handle our questions.

The Promised Land

L ord, make this soda bottle cap say, 'You're a Winner!' If you do this for me, I'll give half of the million dollars to you. For you truly are my lifeline, Lord."

"Lord, help me to find some money, not in a wallet or anything with someone's name on it because then I'd have to return it. Just let it float down from heaven, you know, like manna, only green. And don't have it land too far from me. I worked out last night at that new gym I just joined and my muscles are killing me. If you'll do this for me Lord, I'll give 25 percent right back to you. Well, 15 percent, at least. OK, ten. All right, a love offering. I'll give you a love offering from whatever I have left. Every last bit of the change in my pocket, that's what I'm willing to give you, Lord. And I'm talking the silver coins, too. Not real silver. Those would be collectible. But the rest, all the rest, Lord, are yours. You said 'Ask and you shall receive,' so come on and rain those tens and twenties down on me. Rain 'em down!"

Ah, the promises we make when we want something.

James tells us that one of the reasons we don't receive answers to our prayers is because we pray amiss. We ask out of our own selfish desires, rather than out of true need, or a desire to help others.

There's been a lot of talk about Jabez's prayer lately. Jabez's prayer is found in 1 Chronicles 4:10. It reads like this in the New King James Version, "Oh, that You would bless me indeed, and enlarge my territory, that Your hand would be with me and that You would keep me from evil, that I may not cause pain!"

That's how our prayers should be. Yes, we want God to bless us. Yes, we want him to enlarge our territory of influence, but not so we can forget him. It should be so that we can positively affect the lives of others, and that we would always want him by our side.

Do that and you won't need a bottle cap to tell you you're a winner. In your heart, you'll just know it.

Thoughts to Ponder

When you pray, do you pray like Jabez?

What do you think would be God's purpose if he were to enlarge your territory?

Bumper Sticker for the Day
God meets our needs but hates our greed.

Scripture to Stand On

When you ask, you do not receive, because you ask with wrong motives, that you may spend what you get on your pleasures.

JAMES 4:3

Hello Again, Lord ...

Lord, thank you for not giving me everything I want, but everything I need.

God's No Spin Zone

If you follow politics very much, you've no doubt already discovered there's something called "spinning." Spinning is taking a story and putting our own self-serving angle on it. It's manipulating the truth so that it takes on an entirely different meaning. We tell the story, the truth, but we leave out a few important aspects of that truth. If it's about our opponent or someone we don't care for, we leave out the positive side of the situation. If it's about us, we leave out the negative. It's called "spinning," and it doesn't show up only on the political scene. It shows up in our families, our schools, and even our churches.

Here's how negative spinning works:

If a girl you don't particularly like is late every day to basketball practice and you complain about her to the team, all the while knowing she has to watch her little brother until her mom gets home from work, but you withhold that last bit of information, you're spinning. You're slanting the story to suit your needs—which could be to make the girl look bad in front of the team.

Or maybe you're on the receiving end of a "spin." Say, you're taking your little brother to the zoo, but word gets around that you went to some "wild place where everyone acts like animals, and even dragged your little brother along with you." Everything they're saying is factual, but there's a "spin" on it to make it appear like you did something other than what you did. It took your act of kindness and put a negative spin on it.

Another way to spin the truth would be to complain about someone who has owed you five dollars for two months, but leave out the fact that you took four years to pay back the forty dollars you owed him or her.

See how it works?

We all have a choice as to the kind of spin we put on the things we say. We can try to put people in their best light, or we can fan the flames of innuendo. It really just depends on our motives.

Spinning is what a car tire does in the snow. It may look like it's doing what it's supposed to be doing, but it doesn't get anyone anywhere and just makes a big mess. So does spinning the facts.

Thoughts to Ponder

Think about something you've said recently about a person or a situation. Would you say you told the positive facts, or just the negative ones?

Do you think we tend to judge others most harshly in those areas where we ourselves often fail?

Bumper Sticker for the Day
**Facts are like puzzles. They'll never look right
with only half the pieces.**

Scripture to Stand On

Anyone, then, who knows the good he ought to do and doesn't do it, sins.
JAMES 4:17

Hello Again, Lord ...

Lord, you of all people know what it feels like to have the truth twisted against you. Help me not to do that to others ... friends or enemies.

Horse Sense

It's interesting, isn't it, how in James a comparison is made of our behavior to that of a horse? The analogy is that if a horse has a bit in his mouth, we can make him obey us. Without the bit, however, the horse would have the freedom to wander off wherever he wanted to. He could gallop through the meadow, jump over fences, chase other horses, go outlet shopping. Basically, he could do whatever he wanted ... including getting into trouble. He could gallop right over a cliff. He could try jumping over a fence that's too tall for him, not clear it, and end up breaking his leg. He could chase another horse and find out the horse isn't too happy about it, and then he'd have a fight on his hands, or rather his hooves.

Yet take that same horse, put a bit in his mouth, and he'll do what you want. As long as you control his mouth, he knows who's in charge. He'll go where you lead. He'll stay out of the rapids, out of the cactus patches, and out of the outlet malls.

It's funny to think that the mouth has that much control over the rest of the body, isn't it? Yet it does. Our mouths can get us into things that are none of our business. Our mouths can bring discouragement to others, and to ourselves, too. Our mouths can dash dreams. Our mouths can get facts mixed up and tell them as truth. Our mouths can manipulate. Our mouths can injure someone's spirit. Our mouths can do more damage than we could ever imagine, and some of that damage can go undetected for years. Our mouths can be a real problem, can't they? No wonder James suggested we keep a bit in them.

Thoughts to Ponder

Can you think of a time when your mouth has gotten you into trouble?

Why do you think God wants you to surrender the things you say to his guidance before you speak them?

Bumper Sticker for the Day
He whose mouth is always running is sure to catch it someday.

Scripture to Stand On

When we put bits into the mouths of horses to make them obey us, we can turn the whole animal.

JAMES 3:3

Hello Again, Lord ...

Lord, help me to go where you lead, do what you say, be all you want me to be, and help me to keep my mouth from blocking any of it.

Double Trouble ... and Then Some

Have you ever been in trouble? Really big trouble? I mean, *really, really* big trouble? You did something that you knew you never should have done. Maybe you don't even know why you did it, you just did it. And the next thing you knew you were busted, either by your parents, your teacher, your big brother, or maybe even the police.

Getting into trouble can ruin your day, your week, your year, and in some instances, it can nearly ruin your life.

But God is a God of mercy. You know what he wants us to do when we're faced with trouble in our lives? When we're in that hot water up to our chins? When we're up the creek without a bodyboard?

He wants us to pray.

He wants us to talk to him.

He wants us to tell him all about our situation.

He wants us to trust him.

He wants to help.

It's like when you were a child and climbed up on the kitchen counter and knocked over that cookie jar you were raiding. Your mom and dad were no doubt disappointed in your disobedient behavior, but they probably said, "Come here ..." Then they took you in their arms and lifted you out of the pile of broken glass. You were still in trouble, but they wanted to protect you from your own mess. They wanted to hug you. They wanted to reassure you that even though there would be consequences for your actions, you were still loved.

They wanted you to know that you were better than your failure. They wanted to help you learn from your mistake. They didn't toss you aside, saying, "That's it! We had ordered a perfect child, but obviously we didn't get one. She's going back! She just isn't working out!" Of course not. They still believed in you. They still loved you. You were still their child.

That's how it is with God when we make a mistake. He doesn't toss us aside, either. He doesn't say "Forget it! I thought this one was going to be perfect, but just look how he's acting!" or, "She really failed me this time!"

No, no matter what we've done, God still believes in us. He still loves us. And he wants to help us learn from our mistakes. Instead of leaving us standing there in a pile of broken cookie jar pieces, thinking we're hopeless, God wants us to talk to him so he can reassure us that we're not.

Thoughts to Ponder

How does it make you feel when you get into trouble, and someone still believes in the good inside you?

How does it make you feel to know that God always believes in the good inside you?

Bumper Sticker for the Day
God—our best defense attorney.

Scripture to Stand On

Is any one of you in trouble? He should pray.

JAMES 5:13

Hello Again, Lord ...

Lord, thank you for being there with me even in the middle of the broken cookie jars of life.

Equal Opportunity God

When James talks about favoritism, he's not saying that you can't have a best friend who is closer to you than your other friends. That's perfectly normal. We all have our closest friends, friends who we just enjoy hanging around with more than others.

The favoritism James is referring to is when we don't treat people equally in general. For example, if your drama teacher is always casting the same girl in the class play because her father is wealthy and makes large donations to your school, that's favoritism. If you stop talking to your not-so-popular friend because the popular crowd just came on the scene and you'd rather talk to them, that's favoritism.

God doesn't want us excluding people simply because they are different from us. He wants us to treat each other equally.

Your drama teacher should cast whoever is the best actor for the role in your school play. If you're talking to an unpopular friend when your popular friends walk up to you, introduce everyone and continue the conversation, being careful to include everybody. Who knows? Your popular friends just might learn to like him or her. And if not, at least you'll know you did the right thing.

Equality isn't anything new. It was being addressed thousands of years ago. The fact that it's mentioned numerous times in the Bible must mean that God is trying to tell us something. He doesn't want us playing favorites with his creation.

When you think about it, we wouldn't want him playing favorites with us, either.

Thoughts to Ponder

Have you ever been guilty of favoritism?

Why do you think it's important to treat everyone equally?

Bumper Sticker for the Day
Labels are for merchandise, not people.

Scripture to Stand On

My brothers, as believers in our glorious Lord Jesus Christ, don't show favoritism.

JAMES 2:1

Hello Again, Lord ...

Lord, thank you for never excluding me. Help me to not exclude others, either.

Have a Fun Life

Idon't think I've ever seen a sad baby. Babies come into the world ready to smile and coo and laugh.

But then something happens. They get picked on a little too much in their adolescent years, they fall down one too many times in their teen years, and the next thing you know that cute little smile might not seem so bright anymore.

God intended for us to be happy. He designed our faces to smile. He gave us a mind capable of developing our natural sense of humor. He gave us strong stomach muscles so we could easily handle all those belly laughs that he had planned for us. He wants us to be joyful. Why? Because everything is going to go perfectly in our lives? Of course not. God wouldn't have given us tear ducts if we weren't designed to handle a little sorrow, too. But God knew we'd need the ability both to smile and to cry, so he made us capable of handling both emotions.

I've often said that life is like an EKG. It's going to have plenty of ups and downs for each one of us. If it ever stays level for too long, we better check our pulse, because we could be flatlining. The ups and downs of life let us know we're still here. One day everything can go our way, the next day, nothing does. That's life. Don't expect it to be anything else.

God wants us to be happy in spite of whatever circumstances we might be going through. He wants us to smile in the middle of the storm. If we wait until after it's over, there might be another one on the way and we'll never get the chance to smile. And if we worry that another storm is on its way, we'll never relax enough to enjoy the calm.

So use your laughing muscles as often as you can. Enjoy your good times. And if some bad times come, you can still have joy because God is faithful. And that's certainly something to smile about.

Thoughts to Ponder

Do you think you laugh enough?

Why do you think God wants you to laugh and enjoy the blessings he's given to you?

Bumper Sticker for the Day
Let my people laugh.

Scripture to Stand On

Is anyone happy? Let him sing songs of praise.

JAMES 5:13b

Hello Again, Lord ...

Lord, thank you for giving us a secret weapon against life's troubles—laughter.

Financial Statements

When I was a teenager, I remember the church bus would pick my sisters and me up for Wednesday night youth service. We lived about a half hour from the church, and the bus would pick us up in front of the corner drug store. The bus made several stops through our valley; ours was its first.

One night, after the bus driver had picked up some teenagers from a more affluent section of town, he announced that he had to stop by his house to pick up something. When we pulled up to his house, I'll never forget the comment one of those youth made.

"You call that a house?" she laughed.

The bus driver didn't hear it, of course, but I felt bad for him. Here was a man donating his time to drive around and pick up teenagers for church, and that's the nicest this teenager could be to him?

When God blesses us with financial blessings, it's not to flaunt it in the face of those who have less.

The same thing happens in some social circles at school:

"Can you believe she dresses like that? When's she going to buy something new?"

"If those were the best shoes I could afford, I think I'd go barefoot."

"I hear her family's having money problems. Her dad got fired and her mom's on unemployment. What losers!"

People who criticize this harshly could quickly find themselves on the receiving end of some of those criticisms. God has a way of turning the tables on the prideful.

So, if you're blessed, count your blessings and give God credit. If you're just barely making ends meet, count your blessings and thank God for making those ends meet. God is a good God. When you consider the fact that the greatest treasure in all the world is what's waiting for each of us in eternity, what does it matter who has more in his or her wallet here?

Thoughts to Ponder

How important are material things to you?

Write down five areas in which God has been meeting your needs.

Bumper Sticker for the Day
**All the money in the world can't buy what
God's already given you.**

Scripture to Stand On

Suppose a man comes into your meeting wearing a gold ring and fine clothes, and a poor man in shabby clothes also comes in. If you show special attention to the man wearing fine clothes and say, "Here's a good seat for you," but say to the poor man, "You stand there" or "Sit on the floor by my feet," have you not discriminated among yourselves and become judges with evil thoughts?

JAMES 2:2-4

Hello Again, Lord ...

Lord, thank you for the blessings you've given me—both the ones that I can see and the ones that are intangible.

Problems, Problems, Problems

Envy and selfish ambition have been causing problems since the beginning of man. Remember Adam and Eve? It didn't matter that they could eat of every fruit in the Garden of Eden except for the fruit of the Tree of Knowledge of Good and Evil. That wasn't good enough. They couldn't resist the temptation to eat of that tree, too, and their selfish ambition cost them their home and brought sin into the world.

Remember their children, Cain and Abel? Cain killed Abel in a jealous rage. Jealous over what? Over God's love, believe it or not. Cain knew God was more pleased with Abel's sacrifice, because Abel gave his best and it was true sacrifice. So Cain killed Abel. Rather than improve his own behavior, he got rid of his competition. This was the first family on earth, and already they were dysfunctional.

God created each one of us with free will. We have a choice in the things we do. We can let jealousy rule us, or we can rule over jealousy. We can let selfish ambition be in control of our lives and decisions, or we can be in control of our selfish ambition. The choice is ours. We can be governed by God's boundaries, or we can yield to temptation and end up like Adam and Eve and Cain.

If you think about it, many of the problems that society faces today have envy and selfish ambition at the root. This man wants what that man has, this girl will do anything to get what she desires, the CEO of this company will undermine the CEO of that company to run him out of business, this girl will gossip about that girl in an attempt to throw a student body election. The scenarios are endless.

So, how do you know when someone is acting out of selfish ambition or jealousy? Usually, these behaviors will bring disorder into your life. Maybe you just passed the tryouts for your school's drill team, but instead of being excited for you, a "friend" discourages you from going on to the semifinals. "You won't make it. Don't even try," he or she tells you, day after day after day. Now, you're not sure what to do. You were excited, even hopeful, but now you're confused. Jealousy causes disorder.

Or maybe a classmate steals the answers to the math final, but talks you into taking the blame for it because with something like that on his record, he'll never get into a good college. You're torn between being used and losing a friend. Selfish ambition causes disorder.

We can even bring disorder into our own lives. Maybe we're trying too hard to get the things we want, or we're envious of what someone else has.

Once again, James is telling us to check the motives of others, and reminding us to check our own motives, too. If these things were a problem for God's very first children, and he had to send them out of the garden, then it's safe to say he's pretty serious about not wanting to find the same motives in us.

Thoughts to Ponder

Have you ever been hurt by someone's envy or self-centeredness?

Why do you think these two sins can be so destructive to us?

Bumper Sticker for the Day
The Lord is my shepherd, I shall not want, and want, and want ...

Scripture to Stand On

For where you have envy and selfish ambition, there you find disorder and every evil practice.

JAMES 3:16

Hello Again, Lord ...

Lord, teach me to be content with all that you've already blessed me with, and protect me from the envy or selfish ambition of others.

Free Means Free

Monday—school, biology homework, send "We Missed You" cards to youth who missed last week's youth service.

Tuesday—school, finish short story for English class, church basketball team practice, drama meeting.

Wednesday—school, work on science project, help with youth bake sale after midweek church service.

Thursday—school, study for history test, choir practice.

Friday—school, dentist appointment, play drums for youth group meeting.

Saturday—help with sister's Little League car wash, visit Aunt Betty at the convalescent home, drama practice.

Sunday—teach third-graders' Sunday school, help with church nursery during Sunday morning service, sell tickets to youth spaghetti dinner.

Sound like your schedule? Do you find yourself going in dozens of different circles just trying to get everything done that you need to get done "for the Lord"? If you're doing it because you enjoy staying this busy, that's fine, provided you can handle it and your schoolwork isn't suffering. But if you're keeping this kind of schedule in order to earn God's love, then you're trying to do the impossible, and the unnecessary. None of us have to earn God's love. We can't go to enough church services, help out with enough youth meetings, sell enough candy bars, or rock enough babies in the church nursery, to earn what God has already given to us.

If we're so busy doing "God's business" that we're bitter and miserable, complaining every chance we get about all the things we have "to do for the Lord," then we're working for the wrong reasons. Again, James is asking us to check our motives. God wants our service to be true service, not drudgery. He wants our faithfulness to be true faithfulness, not a feeling of being trapped in an obligation. He wants our works to come naturally, out of a love for him, instead of out of a desire to be noticed.

If you're working for the right reason, you won't feel slighted when you are overlooked for that choir solo, or asked to sit out the first half of a basketball game (even if you're the star player) so one of the less experienced players can have a chance to play. If your motives are right, you'll be able to accept those tough choices between two right things because you don't want to get resentful. If your motives are right, you'll be able to give an anonymous gift to someone and not worry about receiving any credit. If your motives are right, you won't have to think about how many good works you're doing. You'll just do them and let God keep track.

Thoughts to Ponder

Have you ever felt like you were trying to earn God's love by the good things you were doing?

Can you earn God's love, or is it a free gift?

Bumper Sticker for the Day
Work for the Lord, but not for his love.
You already have it.

Scripture to Stand On

Humbly accept the word planted in you, which can save you.

JAMES 1:21b

Hello Again, Lord ...

Thank you, Lord, for the gift of your love. May I never take it for granted or think I have to earn it.

Fanning the Flames

Why do you think James spent so much time dealing with the subject of gossip? To dedicate this many verses to it, you would think he had been hurt or directly affected by gossip in some way, wouldn't you?

As I said before, James is considered to be the author of the Book of James. The Book of James was written between forty and sixty years after the death of his brother, Jesus.

Think about it—James had heard his brother called a lunatic, a blasphemer, and who knows what else, both before and after Jesus' death. By whom? By the same people who, until a week before the crucifixion, had called him their king. People can sure be fickle sometimes, can't they?

Even though this was all part of God's plan, James had to watch how quickly the gossip spread against his brother that final week of his life, and he had to listen to the false accusations and innuendo.

Maybe James even heard a lot of gossip spread about himself and the rest of his family, too.

"I hear the whole family's insane."

"I hear his mother was with child when she married Joseph."

"I hear ..."

As with most gossipers, they just filled in whatever blanks they wanted to.

Make no mistake about it—the crucifixion of Jesus was in God's plan. Nothing would have stopped that. Yet it had to have hurt James to hear the awful things being said and done to his brother.

Maybe that's why he's addressing the power of the tongue here in his writings. He's warning the church of the danger of gossip. He knows firsthand the damage it can do. He's encouraging us to not get caught up in this sinful practice of crucifying people with our tongues. He tells us to encourage and pray for each other instead. He knows the power of that, too.

Thoughts to Ponder

Even though it was in God's plan, how does it make you feel to know the role that gossip and innuendo played in the crucifixion of Jesus?

Can you see why God doesn't want his children participating in that kind of behavior?

Bumper Sticker for the Day
If you can't say something nice, take a vow of silence.

Scripture to Stand On

Likewise the tongue is a small part of the body, but it makes great boasts. Consider what a great forest is set on fire by a small spark.

JAMES 3:5

Hello Again, Lord ...

Lord, help me to see gossip as the fire starter it is.

Sand Castles

G rowing up in Southern California, I used to spend time at the beach. Not a lot of time. I wasn't a surfer or anything like that. (I never learned to swim, and it's hard to hang ten when you're drowning.)

What I enjoyed doing most at the beach, though, was building sand castles. It's fun to build sand castles. Carving out all those tunnels, making staircases and towers and moats and drawbridges. Of course, most of these parts ended up looking nothing like I had envisioned them, but the process was fun.

I have seen some pretty incredible sand castles in my time, though. They were created by people far more talented than I. I've seen some spectacular ones that almost looked good enough to live in. Artisans can do incredible things with sand. I've seen castles, people, cars, planes, and entire villages built out of sand.

As beautiful as they are, though, sand castles are temporary. One good wave can leave them in shambles. Even the most impressive castles won't survive. When the waves rise and the storms come, sand can't stand.

Some of us have lives that look a lot like sand castles. We have the outward appearance of beauty. We have worked hard at it and it truly is something to behold. Everyone who sees it admires it.

But let the first wave of difficulty come along and we collapse. We can't stand because we've built our life out of sand.

Jesus told a parable about a sand castle. He said there were two men who had each built a house. One man built his house on a rock, and the other built his house on sand. When the storm came, the house built on a rock was able to withstand the wind and the waves. The one who had built on sand, couldn't. His house fell down and was washed away.

If things are going smoothly in your life right now, this would be a good time to have a building inspection. What have you been building your life on? Sand? Or Jesus, the Rock of Ages?

You can't stop the storms of life from coming, but like all the sand castles that have ever been built, you don't have to learn the hard way that sand doesn't stand.

Thoughts to Ponder

Would you say you've been building your life on temporal things or eternal things?

Do you feel you'll be able to stand when the next storm comes your way?

Bumper Sticker for the Day
If you want to stand, get out of the sand.

Scripture to Stand On

Religion that God our Father accepts as pure and faultless is this: to look after orphans and widows in their distress and to keep oneself from being polluted by the world.

JAMES 1:27

Hello Again, Lord ...

Lord, help me to build my life on the solid rock of your truth.

The Greed Need

Do you know you don't have to be rich to be a greedy person? Greedy people come with all sizes of bank accounts. In fact, greed has less to do with your net worth than with your attitude.

If people feel the world owes them something, that's greed ... no matter how much or how little money they actually have. Maybe you've met some people like this. They complain about not having any money, but won't do anything to earn any. They sit and wait for success to fall into their laps. Success doesn't fall into laps. It's achieved by hard work and perseverance.

There are also people who pretend to be poor just to get others to pay their way through life. Met any of those? Someone says he can't go on a youth outing because he can't afford it. You feel bad and decide to do without lunch for a few weeks so you can pay his way. He thanks you profusely when you give him the money, but then a few weeks later you find out that he has four thousand dollars in his savings account that he just didn't want to have to dip into. You have $4.86 in your savings account. Suddenly, your sacrifice doesn't feel so good anymore, does it? You were just taken advantage of, and while God will still bless your good intentions, this person's selfishness leaves a bad taste in your mouth. Yet it's even more than selfishness. What people like this are doing is sin, because pretending to be poor when you're not robs from those who really need it.

Greed can also be coveting. Instead of being happy about your friend's new dress, you have to have one just like it or better. That's coveting.

Greed can be manipulating people so they'll give you what you want. "If you don't let me borrow money to get that new CD, then you're not my friend."

There are plenty of other ways to exhibit greed, but they all come from self-centeredness, and we don't have to be rich to have that problem.

Thoughts to Ponder

Can you think of a time when you might have acted out of greed?

Have you ever sacrificed for someone only to find out that person had his or her own money all along? How did it make you feel?

Bumper Sticker for the Day
**The difference between "greed" and "need"
is a lot more than three letters.**

Scripture to Stand On

You have lived on earth in luxury and self-indulgence. You have fattened yourselves in the day of slaughter.

JAMES 5:5

Hello Again, Lord ...

Lord, if I'm going to indulge myself in anything, may it be in your Word.

Wrong Turns

If a car is inadvertently driven onto a field, does that make it a tractor? Of course not. It's still a car, even though it's now being driven alongside a herd of cattle. (Sounds like my first driving test, but I digress.)

Driving a car on an open field won't be a smooth ride. You might even blow a tire or two, and the car will certainly look worse for the wear, but whether it's being driven on a smooth highway or a bumpy field, a car is still a car.

The driver would never say, "Oh, no, look what I've done! I made a wrong turn. Now, I've got a tractor instead of a car!"

That'd be ridiculous, wouldn't it?

No matter where that car goes, it's still a car. If it ends up in a pond, it doesn't become a canoe, or, depending on how deep the pond is, a submarine. It's a car. Even if you find catfish in the glove compartment, it's still a car. All the wrong turns in the world aren't going to change that fact.

Do you know that you are who you are, too, no matter how many wrong turns you make? Wrong turns don't define you or alter your true identity. You may get some wear and tear because of that wrong turn, but you're still you. You have the same qualities you've always had. You're still valuable. And you're still loved. Surely by your family. Surely by your true friends. And certainly by God.

A car doesn't turn into a tractor by making a wrong turn, and a wrong turn doesn't change a person's worth, either.

Thoughts to Ponder

How does it make you feel to know that God still loves you in spite of your wrong turns?

What do you think defines your worth in God's eyes? Your own goodness or his mercy?

Bumper Sticker for the Day
I can't see your failures when your potential is blinding me.

Scripture to Stand On

We all stumble in many ways.

JAMES 3:2a

Hello Again, Lord ...

Lord, thank you that when I add your mercy, you subtract my mistakes and multiply your forgiveness.

No Conditions

Unconditional love is hard to fathom, isn't it? We understand it in part, but it's too amazing to fully comprehend. Most of us grow up thinking if we do A, B, C, or D, people will love us. If they don't, then we add E, F, and G to the list. If that doesn't do it, H, I, and J get thrown in. We're exhausted with all our performing, but we still don't give up. We tell ourselves if we try just a little bit harder, give just a little more, go that extra mile or two or three, we can earn someone's love. When we don't, we try adding K, L, M, and all the rest of the alphabet. We do everything we possibly can. Sometimes it works and sometimes it doesn't.

But we don't have to do anything to get Jesus to love us. His love isn't based on our performance. It isn't subject to what we do or don't do for it. We can't earn it, win it, or even lose it. He won't take it away when we mess up, and none of us will ever be or do enough good to deserve it.

God's love is unconditional. We don't have to do A, B, C, or even Z. He loves us, no matter what.

Unconditional love is hard to fathom, isn't it?

Thoughts to Ponder

How does it make you feel when someone puts conditions on his or her love?

How does it make you feel to know that God loves you uncon-
ditionally?

Bumper Sticker for the Day
Are you working for God's love or living in it?

Scripture to Stand On

The Lord is full of compassion and mercy.

JAMES 5:11

Hello Again, Lord ...

Lord, thank you for making your love affordable. Help me to
remember that even though it's free to us, it cost you everything.

Taking the Plunge

I'm not a very good swimmer. I do all right as long as I stay by the side of the pool, with the security of the cement edge well within my reach. Get me out into deep water, though, and I'm like a homesick Texan. I start heading southward fast.

South isn't the best direction for swimmers.

I know I'd be a better swimmer if I got more practice swimming in the deeper water (or at least beyond the steps), but my fear keeps me from doing that. As long as I stay in the shallow water, though, I'm never going to learn to swim.

Children and babies learn how to swim by going into water that's well over their heads. With enough swimming lessons behind them, and their swim instructor or parent standing nearby, these youngsters are coaxed into jumping right into the pool and then, to their own amazement, swimming to safety.

Like a loving parent, God is never far from our side. But for our own good he wants us to learn how to swim. He wants us to know we can trust him no matter how deep the water gets. Maybe that's why he allows difficulties to flow into our lives from time to time. It forces us to swim and it puts within us the confidence that God will never leave us alone.

People have been known to drown in shallow water, too. So the trick isn't staying in a safe place. It's learning how to swim in all depths of water.

Thoughts to Ponder

Which do you prefer to do—paddle by the steps or swim with the Master?

If you're in deep waters right now, what do you think you're learning from this experience?

Bumper Sticker for the Day
Learn to swim, but stay close to the lifeguard.

Scripture to Stand On

Why, you do not even know what will happen tomorrow. What is your life? You are a mist that appears for a little while and then vanishes.
JAMES 4:14

Hello Again, Lord ...

Thank you, Lord, for being someone I can trust in the shallow waters, the deep waters, and everything in between.

Equal Time

Wow! That was Pastor Rick's best sermon! I never realized how much God hated prejudice."

"That's what he talked about?"

"You were sitting right behind me. Weren't you listening?"

"I got stuck next to those nerdy Mitchell brothers. The only thing I heard was the sound of my reputation going down in flames.... So it was a really good sermon, huh?"

"Yeah, it was about how we should treat everyone equally, you know, not show favoritism."

"Man, I wish I had heard it, but I just couldn't concentrate. I hate sitting next to those two. They're such losers. When are the ushers gonna divide the church into two parts—the cool section and the un-cool section? I put it in the suggestion box weeks ago, but they haven't done it yet. That'd solve everything.... So you were saying ... ?"

"Uh ... never mind."

"No, really. I want to know. It sounds like it was a really good sermon."

"Well, basically he talked about how we're all equal in God's sight. So I guess you could say God loves the Mitchell brothers just as much as he loves you and me."

"Oh, please."

"I'm serious. That's what the pastor said. He read it right out of the Bible."

"Really? Hmmm.... Well, then, I guess it's time for a change."

"You're gonna drop all those labels that you've been putting on people and start treating the Mitchell brothers just like you would anyone else?"

"Are you kidding? I'm changing churches!"

Sometimes we're the last one to see our own prejudices, aren't we?

Thoughts to Ponder

Is there someone at your school or church who is being treated unfairly because of their outward appearance or social status?

In what ways could you be a friend to him or her?

Bumper Sticker for the Day
In God's eyes, division never adds up.

Scripture to Stand On

But if you show favoritism, you sin and are convicted by the law as lawbreakers.

JAMES 2:9

Hello Again, Lord ...

Lord, thank you for giving us all the same opportunity to have you in our lives.

A Jesus Kind of Friend

Jesus is a special kind of friend. He'll see the best in you even when you're not showing it.

He'll never call you names.

He'll sit with you when you don't know a soul in the cafeteria.

He won't turn his back on you even after you tell him to leave.

If you get into trouble, he'll remind you of your worth then stay and sit in detention with you.

He'll be the same friend to your face as he is behind your back.

He'll be your moral support during that oral report.

He'll show up when you least expect it and when you most want him to.

He'll assure you that you can do it even when you're convinced you can't.

He'll let you make your own decisions, but won't abandon you when you've made a wrong one.

He'll give you a reason to laugh.

He'll make you want to change.

He won't keep score of the times you've let him down.

He won't keep count of your failures.

He won't keep track of how much you owe him.

He won't betray your confidence.

He won't abuse you.

He won't take you for granted.

He'll still be there when everyone else has left.

Jesus is a special kind of friend.

Thoughts to Ponder

What kind of friend has Jesus been to you?

What kind of friend have you been to Jesus?

Bumper Sticker for the Day
With Jesus you're never a party of one.

Scripture to Stand On

Mercy triumphs over judgment!

JAMES 2:13b

Hello Again, Lord ...

Lord, thank you for showing us what friendship is all about.

Closed for Business

Uh-oh. Another scripture on the tongue. It seems like the book of James is really trying to get a message across to us, doesn't it?

Maybe that's because Christians in James' day, like many of us today, looked at gossip as one of the "acceptable sins." They knew about God's Big Ten—the Thou Shalt Nots that he handed down to Moses—but gossip wasn't that big a deal. Right? I mean, no one went to jail for gossip. No one was ostracized from society because of gossip. So it must be OK.

Well, after you read the Book of James you can't deny that God is expressing to us over and over and over again his disdain for gossip. It's wrong, and it's sin.

One of the main dangers of gossip is that it travels so fast. The speed of light and the speed of sound are nothing compared to the speed of gossip. Sir Winston Churchill once said, "A lie gets halfway around the world before the truth has a chance to get its pants on."

Maybe the reason gossip travels so quickly is that it's not usually weighed down by very much, if any, truth. Gossip needs only to "sound" true. Most gossipers don't check out their sources or ask the victim whether or not a story is true. They just receive it, add to it, and send it on its merry way. When something travels that quickly, it's virtually impossible for the victim to ever completely straighten out the mess it causes. How does a person clear up his or her name when he or she doesn't even know who has participated in the gossip fest?

God deals with those who are addicted to gossip pretty severely here in the book of James. And it is an addiction. By gossiping, the gossipers are fulfilling a need to make them feel better about themselves. Usually it comes from jealousy. "If I can bring this person down, I'll look more spiritual."

Yet in God's eyes, nothing could be farther from the truth.

James is warning us about the dangers of the tongue. There are a lot of chapters in this devotional dedicated to the tongue because there are a lot of verses pertaining to it. Gossip is wrong. Maybe we should start seeing it for what it is.

Thoughts to Ponder

What do you do when you hear something negative about someone you know? Do you listen and spread it, or do you go to that person to find out the truth?

Other than jealousy, what do you think motivates someone to gossip about someone else?

Bumper Sticker for the Day
Gossip can't travel unless we give it legs.

Scripture to Stand On

Take ships as an example. Although they are so large and are driven by strong winds, they are steered by a very small rudder wherever the pilot wants to go.

JAMES 3:4

Hello Again, Lord ...

Lord, whenever I hear gossip, give me the courage to correct the story if I know the truth, and if I don't, give me the courage to correct the gossiper and find out the truth.

How to Succeed by Getting F's

Sound ridiculous? Of course it does. After all, an "F" isn't the grade you want to see on your report card, is it?

Yet you really can succeed in life by scoring "F's"—if they're the right kind of "F's."

The most important "F" is faith. Faith isn't tangible. You can't touch it. You can't buy it on eBay. It's not pitched on an infomercial. It's something that's inside of you. Faith helps you believe that there's a bigger purpose for your life than just getting up every morning and going to bed every night. It helps you believe the best of people when they're showing only their worst. It helps you believe there's a bigger picture than what you happen to be seeing at the moment. And it helps you know that there is a God who created all things, and that he cares for you.

The next "F" is friendship. We all need friends. Yet some of us, even some of us Christians, don't know how to be a true friend. We need to pattern the friendship we offer others after the friendship God offers us. If it measures up, then we're doing it right.

Another "F" to shoot for is focus. Don't get sidetracked with discouragement, pettiness, greed, impatience, or any of the other things that can get in the way of God's will for your life.

There's also an "F" for freedom. Freedom to make our own choices, good or bad, and to learn from them. That's one of the secrets to success. If you achieve only what other people want you to achieve, you won't be a true success. You may make plenty of money, but you'll always have a feeling of unfulfillment, because those weren't your dreams, they were someone else's. Pursue your dreams in accordance with God's plan for your life, and no matter what happens, you'll be a success, because you didn't fail God or yourself.

One more "F" you can earn is fairness. Be fair to those around you. Don't expect behavior from them that you're overlooking in yourself. Be fair. Life may not be fair, but we certainly can try to be.

Forgiveness is another "F" that you will want to achieve. To truly succeed in life, you need the forgiveness of God, you need to forgive others, and you need to forgive yourself.

Another "F" is for foundation. You need a good foundation to succeed in life. Then, when things don't go right in your life (and you can't get through life without having something go wrong), you won't be shaken.

Finally, the last "F" is for fun. Life is too unbearable without this "F." You have to have fun, you have to laugh, you have to sing, you have to play if you're going to make it. So get the best grades you can in school, but in life, remember it's good to get as many of the above "F's" as possible.

Thoughts to Ponder

How do you think you would be graded in faith? Forgiveness? Fairness? Friendship? Fun?

Why does God wants us to enjoy the life he's given to us?

Bumper Sticker for the Day
The report card that really counts is the one we get in life.

Scripture to Stand On

Who is wise and understanding among you? Let him show it by his good life, by deeds done in the humility that comes from wisdom.

JAMES 3:13

Hello Again, Lord ...

Lord, help me to remember that, just like with my schoolwork, I'm going to get out of life what I put into it.

Life Rage

Every once in awhile the news will carry a story of someone who had a fit of road rage and attacked another motorist. Sitting in bumper-to-bumper traffic, dealing with inconsiderate drivers, a broken air conditioner on an unusually hot day—all of these can throw people into a fit if they're not careful.

Yet road rage isn't the only thing that can cause us to lose our tempers. How about Locker Rage? Ever have a lock freeze up on you when you've got thirty seconds to get to class? Ever have all your books come tumbling out of your locker, landing right on top of your foot that's already in an Ace bandage from a soccer injury? Ever rise up from getting your things out of a bottom locker only to hit your head on the corner of the open locker door above you?

And how about Lost Homework Rage? That's the rage you can get into when you can't find your homework, or when your dog really did eat it and you know your teacher is never going to believe you.

Then there's the Can't Go to the Party Friday Night Rage, the Grounding Rage, the Missed Telephone Call Rage, the Someone Used All the Shampoo Rage, the Where's the Remote Control Rage, the Who Recorded over My Favorite Music Video Rage, the Why'd I Get a Blemish on Picture Day Rage, and so many more.

Rages are unfair to the people around you, and to yourself. No one should have to suffer for your bad day. If you allow yourself to go into a rage, then you're only making the problem worse. Furthermore, the rage could be coming from a different place entirely. It might not have anything to do with your homework, your locker, that missed telephone call, or any of the other reasons you think you're upset. It might be about something totally different, a problem you may not be wanting to face, a difficult situation that hasn't been confronted yet, a hurt that hasn't healed, or who knows what else?

So the next time you get angry, ask yourself what it is that's really bothering you. Is it the locker, or is it a strained relationship? Is it that blemish, or is it low self-esteem? Raging doesn't help anyone's day. But finding out what's going on inside you can definitely change your perspective. Maybe even your life.

Thoughts to Ponder

How much does it take to throw you into a rage?

Have you ever gotten angry over something small when you knew down deep it was really about something else?

Bumper Sticker for the Day
Some wounds heal faster in the sunlight.

Scripture to Stand On

For man's anger does not bring about the righteous life that God desires.

JAMES 1:20

Hello Again, Lord ...

Lord, help me to examine my life to find those areas of hurt or frustration that I've been hiding.

Wise Guy

Do you know God will give you wisdom if you ask for it? Now, before you get excited, I should explain that this doesn't mean you can bypass studying for that biology exam, then pray and expect God to miraculously tell you the correct scientific name for every body part of an armadillo. What it does mean is that he will give you wisdom for making those difficult decisions, like whether to go bowling or stay home and study for that biology exam.

Wisdom isn't our ticket to slack off in our academics. We need to know history, grammar, science, and all the other subjects required by our schools. An education in those areas is what will keep us from being in a discussion about Thomas Jefferson someday and asking, "Wasn't he a rock singer from the sixties?"

Wisdom, on the other hand, isn't book smarts. It might not get you the big money on *Jeopardy*, or give you a shot on *Who Wants to Be A Millionaire?* The Board of Education will probably never give you a test to find out your Wisdom Quotient, and wisdom isn't something in which you can get a degree at Harvard.

Yet, the more wisdom you have, the more your friends will come to you for advice. The more wisdom you have, the better your own choices are going to be. The more wisdom you have, the more successful you're going to be in life.

Wisdom is good judgment. It's knowing how to decide between a right choice and a wrong choice. It's also knowing how to decide between two good choices. It's knowing what to say and what not to say. It's knowing how to deal with difficult people without losing your own rights in the process. It's discernment. It's common sense. It's the ability to learn from past mistakes. It's the ability to learn from other people's mistakes. It's seeing through the spin, the hype, the manipulation, the drama, and finding the truth of a matter. It's knowing there are two sides of a story. It's being smart enough not to be used by those who are very convincing and very wrong. It's insight. It's understanding. Wisdom is heart knowledge. And it's a gift from God.

Solomon was considered the wisest man in the world. When two women were brought before him, both claiming to be the mother of the same baby, he didn't take anyone's word for it. He simply suggested that they divide the baby in two, giving one side to each woman. Solomon wouldn't have done this, I'm sure, but he knew that the real mother would never allow such a thing to happen to her child. She would gladly sacrifice if it meant saving her child's life. The real mother relinquished her claim on her baby, and then Solomon knew which lady was the real mother and which one was the jealous imposter.

Pretty smart. That's wisdom.

God wants to give you wisdom in all the areas of your life. In your relationships. In your career choices. In your job search. In your decision as to which college to attend. God wants to be your life tutor. He's ready to give you all the wisdom you want and need. All you have to do is ask for it.

Thoughts to Ponder

Could you use more wisdom?

Why do you think God wants to give us his wisdom?

Bumper Sticker for the Day
God loves a wise guy (and girl, too).

Scripture to Stand On

If any of you lacks wisdom, he should ask God, who gives generously to all without finding fault, and it will be given to him.

JAMES 1:5

Hello Again, Lord ...

Lord, give me wisdom ... and I could use some help in history class, too.

Why Me, Lord?

Have you ever been in the midst of a crisis and found your-self thinking, *God, why are you doing this to me?* When something goes wrong in our lives, it's human nature to blame God. After all, he's God ... he could stop it from happening if he really wanted to, right? He could make your sister get off drugs and bring harmony into your home again. He could have kept your father from being hit by that reckless driver. He could get those bullies to stop picking on you at school, or maybe even at church. He could have blocked the events of 9-11 from ever happening. He's all-powerful. He's all-know-ing. He's God, and he loves us.

So why doesn't he stop these bad things from happening?

Because he created man with free will. It's as simple and as complicated as that. We have the free will to make our own choices, and we human beings don't always make the best ones.

But in James, God warns us about blaming him for the dif-ficult circumstances in our lives. God isn't causing your sister to take drugs. He's not making those bullies at school pick on you. He didn't make that car hit your father. And he certainly wasn't responsible for 9-11. God is a good God. He does good things to us and for us. He wants the best for our lives and loves us more than we could ever imagine. He can and wants to bring peace into our homes. He certainly can heal our brother, but if he doesn't, then he has another plan and we have to trust him. He doesn't approve of bullies picking on us, but that's their bad behavior, not his. And those kids at church that might be snubbing us? God's telling us here in James that blaming him is wrong, so why do it? People have choices, and sometimes even Christians don't make the right ones.

One good thing that does come out of difficult times, though, is spiritual and emotional growth. You can't go through a difficult period and not change. Struggle, loss, and hurt will make you a different person. Deeper, stronger, better. One day you might be able to speak up for others who are facing bullies, or comfort someone whose family member is fighting for his or her life, or encourage someone else whose sibling may be struggling with drugs. God isn't responsible for your difficulties, but if you let him, he will use those experiences for good.

Life is life. God never promised that it would be anything else. But he is a good God and he's promised to walk through life with us, every step of the way. It's as simple and as complicated as that.

Thoughts to Ponder

Have you ever unfairly blamed God for a difficulty in your life?

In what ways do you think God is showing you his love even in spite of your circumstances?

Bumper Sticker for the Day
God is good. Case closed.

Scripture to Stand On

When tempted, no one should say, "God is tempting me." For God cannot be tempted by evil, nor does he tempt anyone.

JAMES 1:13

Hello Again, Lord ...

Forgive me, Lord, when I unfairly blame you for life's difficulties, and for when I forget to thank you for life's blessings.

The Whole Picture

The next time you watch a movie or television show, stare at the bottom righthand corner of the screen. Fixate on it. Block out everything that's happening on the rest of the screen. Only see what's happening in that corner and nothing else.

Do you think you'll enjoy the movie very much? Do you think you'll miss any of the plot, the action, the humor? Do you think your neck is going to be sore?

It would be ridiculous to do something like that, wouldn't it? When you watch a movie, your eyes want to take in the whole screen, not just a corner of it. By watching everything on the screen, the movie makes sense, the action is meaningful, the humor works.

That's how it is with life. Too often we fixate on just a corner of what's happening in our lives and either don't want to see the whole picture or forget that there is one. But when we view our life just one corner at a time, nothing makes much sense.

By pulling back and looking at the whole picture, however, we realize there's a lot more happening than what's taking place in that little corner at this particular time. There's the big picture, and while the corner doesn't make sense, the big picture does. We can relax knowing that from God's point of view, everything is flowing together nicely, making the story of our lives. And even with all the plot twists and turns, if we know God, ultimately, there will be a happy ending.

So the next time you find yourself focusing too much on just a little corner of your life, take a moment to stand back and look at the big picture. The big picture is what counts. The big picture is what will someday be a great story.

Thoughts to Ponder

Is there a corner of your story that you've been focusing on too much lately?

When you stand back and look at the big picture of your life, does that corner seem less significant?

Bumper Sticker for the Day
For a clear picture of life, keep your focus on God.

Scripture to Stand On

Be patient, then, brothers, until the Lord's coming. See how the farmer waits for the land to yield its valuable crop and how patient he is for the autumn and spring rains.

JAMES 5:7

Hello Again, Lord ...

Lord, thank you for seeing, and loving, the whole me.

Testing, Testing

Want to know if your actions are coming from a Godly place, or if they're coming from somewhere else? Put them to the test.

Are they pure?
Are they peace-loving?
Are they considerate?
Are they submissive?
Are they full of mercy?
Are they full of good fruit?
Are they impartial?
Are they sincere?

If you didn't answer yes to each of these, then your actions may not be as holy or right or justified as you may have thought.

Ouch.

Did God really say that?

He really did. So let's take a look at them one by one.

First, are your actions pure? This is a simple one to test. All you have to do is honestly look at your motives. Why are you really doing what you're doing? Are you trying to be noticed? Are you trying to gain friends?

Are your actions peace-loving? Are you thinking of the other person's peace, or just your own? Do you truly want peace, or do you enjoy conflict?

Are your actions considerate? If you're not listening to anyone else's side of the story, how can you say you're being considerate?

Are your actions submissive? Are you being submissive to those in authority? To your parents? To God?

Are your actions full of mercy? It doesn't matter how right you are, if your actions are not coming from a place of mercy, or if you're just wanting to prove the wrongness of the other person, then it's not a godly action. A merciful heart doesn't secretly rejoice over the pain of others.

Are your actions full of good fruit? Will good come out of your actions, or more tension and stress?

Are your actions impartial? Are you looking at the whole picture as an outsider would, or are you acting out of bias?

Are your actions sincere? God saved this one for last because none of the above mean anything if you're faking it all. Remember, God knows your heart. You can fool other people by pretending to be peace-loving, but if you're a barracuda in private, don't you think God knows that? If you do good only in order to be noticed by others, don't you think God sees that, too?

Always put your actions to God's test. If they don't pass, change them. If they do, you're an "action" hero.

Thoughts to Ponder

Think of a situation with which you had to deal recently. If you put your actions to this test, how would they measure up?

Why do you think you need to understand the real truth behind your actions?

Bumper Sticker for the Day
Before you act, know your motivation.

Scripture to Stand On

But the wisdom that comes from heaven is first of all pure; then peace-loving, considerate, submissive, full of mercy and good fruit, impartial and sincere.

JAMES 3:17

Hello Again, Lord ...

Lord, help me to think about my actions before I act. Life just plays out better that way.

Bird Brain

Around four o'clock every morning the birds outside of our house start singing. It's still dark. No one's awake yet. You can't see flowers, birdhouses, or even a bird's favorite place to hang out—telephone wires. Yet the birds sing as if the sun were already up in the sky. They sing as if the day had already begun. They sing as if everything were perfect.

It's not. It's dark. And everyone's trying to sleep.

But try telling them that.

At first I thought their singing was intrusive. Four o'clock in the morning is too early to listen to birds singing. I'd open one eye, look at the clock, then roll over, bury my head in my pillow, and try to get a few more hours of sleep.

I'm used to it now, though, and I've come to look at it as sort of inspiring. After all, here are a group of birds who, right in the middle of the night, surrounded by darkness everywhere, are singing. Loudly singing. Why? Because they know morning is coming. It's not here yet, but they know it's coming. If yesterday was any proof, and the day before that, and the day before that, morning is just around the corner. And they're so excited about it, they can't help but get a jump on it.

We could learn a lot from birds. When darkness is surrounding us, are we singing? Are we acting on faith that the sun is going to come out again, just as it has every morning of our lives? Or are we waiting for the dawn to actually appear before we dare to sing?

Birds know morning is coming, and they're ready to celebrate it, no matter how dark the sky looks at the moment.

We shouldn't wait for the sun to appear to start our concert either.

Thoughts to Ponder

Do you find it difficult to sing during your dark moments?

Why do you think it's important to anticipate and celebrate each new day?

Bumper Sticker for the Day
Sing until the sun comes up, not only when it comes up.

Scripture to Stand On

Blessed is the man who perseveres under trial, because when he has stood the test, he will receive the crown of life that God has promised to those who love him.

JAMES 1:12

Hello Again, Lord ...

Lord, help me to remember that the sun will shine again, even when all I may see at the moment is darkness.

Do You Mind?

Daydreaming is fun, isn't it? You can let your mind take you wherever you want to go, and you don't even have to pack. You can go to Paris, Rome, the Grammys, the Oscars, the Olympics, a live concert—it doesn't matter. Your mind has the ticket, it's got the backstage passes, it's already won the bronze, the silver, and the gold! There's nothing stopping you!

Enjoy!

You can go shopping in your mind, too, and buy whatever you want. You can drive the hottest car, live in the biggest house, have the best clothes, and never charge a dime to your parents' credit cards.

You can daydream about that cute new guy or girl in your English class. You can pretend you're dating. You can pretend you're engaged. You can pretend whatever you want, because it's just a harmless daydream.

That's true as long as our daydreams are harmless. But if we allow ourselves to get carried away with wrongful desires (lust, greed, revenge, and so on), then they're not so harmless. We risk becoming so obsessed with that desire that it becomes action. And when it becomes action, it becomes sin. Sometimes, even before. Remember when Jesus warned that lusting after someone in your heart is as bad as having committed the sin?

That's why we need to do everything we can to keep our minds fixed on the good and positive things of life. Philippians 4:8 tells us, "Finally, brothers, whatever is true, whatever is noble, whatever is right, whatever is pure, whatever is lovely, whatever is

153

admirable—if anything is excellent or praiseworthy—think about such things."

It's OK to daydream. Where would the arts be without creative, healthy imaginations? But keep your mind pure. You're its keeper. Don't let it go places where it shouldn't go.

Thoughts to Ponder

If someone made a movie of your mind, what kind of rating would it get?

Why do you think it's important for you to guard your thoughts?

Bumper Sticker for the Day
Where your mind goes, the rest of you soon follows.

Scripture to Stand On

Then, after desire has conceived, it gives birth to sin; and sin, when it is full-grown, gives birth to death.

JAMES 1:15

Hello Again, Lord ...

Lord, help me fill my mind with good things so there'll be no room for anything else.

Heart Exam

Have you ever had your heart examined? It usually involves a stethoscope. The doctor places the stethoscope on your chest and listens to your heartbeat. From that, he or she can then determine if there's something that needs closer examination.

If there is, an electrocardiogram, or EKG, might be ordered. An EKG reads your heart's electrical impulses.

For an even closer look, your doctor might also order an echocardiogram. An echocardiogram works with ultrasound to produce a picture of your heart and its chambers. It works in much the same manner as the ultrasound that was used to detect submarines during World War II. An echocardiogram can reveal any structural abnormalities in your heart or the heart valves.

If it looks like your doctor still needs more information, a catheterization might be arranged. A catheterization is a process where a thin catheter is inserted into either your leg or arm and moved into the area of your heart. If the catheterization confirms an abnormality, heart surgery or another form of treatment might then be recommended.

That's how our physical heart problems might be handled. Now, what about our spiritual ones?

Most of us don't look at our spiritual hearts much closer than the stethoscope stage. We take a quick listen, then go on about our day. But God goes deeper than that. He sees beyond the scope of an EKG, an echocardiogram, or even a spiritual catheter. He sees all the way inside, into every chamber of our lives. Nothing escapes his caring eyes. And like the good physician he is, he lets us know what we need to do to take care of the problem areas and be whole again.

Thoughts to Ponder

How long has it been since you've had a spiritual heart exam?

Why do you think it's important not to overlook any corner of your heart?

Bumper Sticker for the Day
God—the world's best heart doctor.

Scripture to Stand On

Anyone who listens to the word but does not do what it says is like a man who looks at his face in a mirror and, after looking at himself, goes away and immediately forgets what he looks like.

JAMES 1:23-24

Hello Again, Lord ...

Thank you, Lord, for helping me keep my "heart" healthy and fit.

And Starring ...

If someone made a movie of your life, how big a part do you think God would get? The lead? A supporting actor role? Or would he just be making a cameo appearance?

The answer depends on the size of the role he's played in your real life, doesn't it? Think about it—have you been including God in every scene of your life, or only those scenes where there's a crisis and he has to come in and "save the day"? Have you been able to hear him when he speaks, or do you and the rest of the cast talk over every line of his dialogue so he can hardly be heard? Did he win the heart of the one he loves or did he get rejected early on in the story? You've been writing the story of your life. The size of God's role in it depends on how big a part you've given him to play.

In case you didn't know it, God doesn't like making cameo appearances in anyone's life. He wants the lead. He wants to direct. He doesn't want his part ending up on the cutting room floor. He doesn't want people talking over his lines. He doesn't want to just show up in a crisis. He wants to be in the whole movie.

If that's not the part you've written for God, maybe it's time for a rewrite.

Thoughts to Ponder

When you think of your life story, would you say it has centered around God, or has he merely been a peripheral character?

Why do you think the story of your life will be more interesting with God playing a major role?

Bumper Sticker for the Day
**When God's the star of your life's movie,
it's guaranteed to be a runaway hit.**

Scripture to Stand On

You believe that there is one God. Good! Even the demons believe that—and shudder.

JAMES 2:19

Hello Again, Lord ...

Forgive me for the times when I've upstaged you, Lord.

Yeah, but She ...

When God confronted Adam and Eve about their disobedience, Adam's first response was, "Yeah, but she ..."

He had fallen, but of course it wasn't his fault.

"It's all her fault, God."

He even tried to dump some of the blame on God.

"It was that woman *you* gave me."

Eve was just as wishy-washy.

"The serpent tempted me."

It was the serpent's fault. It was the woman's fault. It was God's fault. It was Adam's fault. Everyone passed the buck.

Do you know any people like that? Nothing is ever their fault. They'll talk you into doing something you know you shouldn't, then say, "It's your fault for listening to me." They're experts at talking their way out of trouble and talking you into it.

It's dangerous to be friends with people like that. People who'll use you as a scapegoat to their own shortcomings or wrongdoings. Throughout our lives we're going to make enough of our own mistakes to answer for, without having to answer for someone else's.

"She made me do it," and "He made me do it," weren't the answers God was looking for from Adam and Eve. They're not the answers he's looking for from us, either.

Thoughts to Ponder

Would you say you take responsibility for the things you do wrong, or are you a blamer?

How do you feel when someone blames you for something he or she did wrong?

Bumper Sticker for the Day
There are no winners in the blame game.

Scripture to Stand On

But each one is tempted when, by his own evil desire, he is dragged away and enticed.

JAMES 1:14

Hello Again, Lord ...

Lord, when I'm wrong, help me to admit it. When I'm wronged, help others admit it, too.

Believe It or Not

Do you know someone who is so unsure of his or her own opinion that he or she can't make even the slightest decision?

"Should I buy the red shirt or the blue one? Or how 'bout the green one? Never mind, the yellow one is best, I'm sure of it. But then again, what do I know? You make the decision for me."

Stand behind someone like this at an ice cream stand and you'll never get waited on.

"One scoop of cookie dough and one scoop of the strawberry swirl. No, make that one scoop of brownie blast and one scoop of butter pecan. Wait, make that two scoops of pistachio nut and sprinkle some M&M's on top.... On second thought, let's go with one scoop of pineapple sherbet and a scoop of the French vanilla. Then again ..."

Indecisive people can really get on your nerves, can't they?

What's worse, though, are people who are indecisive in what they believe. One day they're unwavering in this belief, the next day they rescind that belief and claim another one. They've got "faith du jour," otherwise known as "faith of the day." They go with whatever belief system is popular at the moment. They're holy chameleons. Their faith takes on a different look depending on who they happen to be with at the moment.

Faith like this rarely survives in a real test.

The minute they are challenged, these people abandon their belief system and rush to a different one. It's like watching a one-man tennis game. They start out on one side of the

162

net, then as soon as they hit the ball, they hop over the net to play that side, too.

God doesn't want us flip-flopping in our faith. He doesn't want us altering our beliefs to go along with the current social or political climate. He wants our faith to be real, to be able to stand in the midst of difficulties, and to be able to last all the years of our lives.

If you're having trouble deciding what you believe, get into the Bible for yourself and find out exactly what it is you believe, and why. There are no winners in a one-man tennis match. It'll only wear you out.

Thoughts to Ponder

Do you have a firm grasp on what you believe?

Why do you think it's important to be unwavering in your faith?

Bumper Sticker for the Day
A double-minded man gets twice the headaches.

Scripture to Stand On

But when he asks, he must believe and not doubt, because he who doubts is like a wave of the sea, blown and tossed by the wind. That man should not think he will receive anything from the Lord; he is a double-minded man, unstable in all he does.

JAMES 1:6-8

Hello Again, Lord ...

Lord, help me to find out for myself what I believe, and not waver.

Double Talk

Would you listen to a personal trainer who was sixty pounds overweight and had a cholesterol level above three hundred tell you how much you need to get in shape, all the while he's washing a brownie down with a chocolate shake?

Would you let a football player who just ran eighty yards to score a touchdown for the opposing team give you tips on how to play football?

How about someone who corrects you for keeping that quarter you found on the sidewalk, while she's slipping the salt and pepper shaker from that fast food restaurant into her purse?

Most of us will listen to good advice, but if the people giving it don't even follow it themselves, it seems kind of pointless, doesn't it?

That's why Jesus came down so hard on the Pharisees. They weren't perfect, but they were blind to their imperfections. They were in desperate need of grace themselves, yet they offered very little of it to others. That's the problem with critical people. They excuse their own bad behaviors while holding other people to the letter of the law. We know how Jesus felt about this kind of attitude then, and it's safe to say he feels the same way about it now.

Thoughts to Ponder

Have you ever been corrected by someone who didn't live up to what he or she was preaching?

Are there any areas in your own life where your walk doesn't quite match up to your talk?

Bumper Sticker for the Day

Perfection—an unattainable goal usually required of others.

Scripture to Stand On

Can both fresh water and salt water flow from the same spring?

JAMES 3:11

Hello Again, Lord ...

Lord, help me to judge my own actions by the same standards with which I judge other people's.

Peace, Please

I hate conflict. I always have. I much prefer peace. If I see conflict coming, I go the other way. I'll put up with an awful lot before I finally say something to whoever it is who is treating me unfairly or causing a disruption in my life.

Maybe I'm nonconfrontational because I'm not very quick at comebacks. By the time it dawns on me that someone has just made a rude comment, that person is usually long gone. And even then I'll give that person the benefit of the doubt until his or her behavior is staring me right in the face and I can't deny it any more.

Do you like your life to stay peaceful, too? Except for a few die-hard bullies who actually enjoy conflict, I think most of us prefer peace.

So does God. He doesn't run from conflict, of course, like we might. He's all-powerful, so he doesn't have to. Yet he does prefer peace. He likes order. If he didn't, why did he put so much order in the universe when he created it? Clearly, God prefers peace. He wants his children to get along. He doesn't like all the bickering and quarreling any more than any other father would.

So, does this mean we should put up with inconsiderate behavior and seek peace at any cost? Should we never stand up for ourselves? Should we let others say and do whatever they want? No, there are certain situations where we have to stand up, where we have to draw a line, where we have to at long last say something to the individual so the negative treatment doesn't continue. That's how that person learns to act better. That's how we learn to speak up. And that's how we can finally have true peace.

Thoughts to Ponder

How do you feel about conflict?

Why do you think that God prefers us to live in peace?

Bumper Sticker for the Day
Give someone a "peace" of your mind.

Scripture to Stand On

Peacemakers who sow in peace raise a harvest of righteousness.

JAMES 3:18

Hello Again, Lord ...

Lord, give me the wisdom to know when I need to face conflict to solve it, and when I need to keep quiet and let it resolve itself.

Iron Man

Do you know we can help each other become better people? Proverbs 27:17 says, "As iron sharpens iron, so one man sharpens another." In other words, we can bring out the best in each other.

James tells us something similar in his writings. He says that we should confess our sins to each other and pray for each other so that we might be healed.

That's what James 5:16 says. Now, let's talk about what it doesn't say.

It doesn't say, "Confess your sins to each other, so that you may hold them against each other and no longer be friends."

It doesn't say, "Confess your sins to each other so you'll have something to bring up in a later argument."

It doesn't say, "Confess your sins to each other so you'll feel better about your own wrongdoings. ('Well, I'm not as bad as he is,' or 'I would never do what she did!')"

It doesn't say, "Confess your sins so that you can talk about them to your other friends over lunch."

It says, "Confess your sins to each other *and* pray for each other so that you may be healed" (Emphasis added).

The healing comes only after the prayer. If you only have confession and sidestep the prayer, nothing will get better. In fact, a whole lot of things might get worse. The trust between you and your friend will be broken. (And trust is a very hard thing to repair.) Your friend's (and possibly your own) reputation will be scarred. And most importantly, the person breaking the confidence will have a false sense of security. You might think that because you don't struggle with the same things that your friend struggles with, God holds you in higher esteem. Yet sin is sin to God, and whether you want to see it or not, gossip is just as wrong as whatever your friend might be struggling with.

Yes, iron sharpens iron, but if you're only hearing a friend's confession, then leaving him or her out in the rain to rust, both your friendship and your witness are going to corrode before you know it.

Thoughts to Ponder

How do you handle confessions that your friends make to you?

Why do you think praying for your friends is better than talking about them?

Bumper Sticker for the Day
Good friends are never afraid of being quoted.

Scripture to Stand On

Therefore confess your sins to each other and pray for each other so that you may be healed. The prayer of a righteous man is powerful and effective.

JAMES 5:16

Hello Again, Lord ...

When my friends trust me with their prayer requests, may I always take the direct road to you, Lord, and not the back road through Gossip Way.

The Unfairness of Pharisees

Modern-day Pharisees are interesting to watch in action, aren't they? They find those areas where they easily excel, then make those their platform for condemning others.

"I certainly don't do that sin," they say piously, diverting everyone's attention from the sins they do commit.

Yet, according to the Book of James, it doesn't matter if someone never steals; if he or she bears false witness about others, that person is just as guilty as a thief. It doesn't matter if a person never tells a lie; if that person harbors hatred in his or her heart toward someone, the Bible says that he or she is guilty of breaking all the other laws.

In other words, what God is telling us is that we aren't perfect. Surprise! Every single one of us has broken God's laws. Yet some people enjoy making us feel like we don't measure up to them, as if there were degrees of sin.

But measure up to what? If we break Laws 1, 2, and 3 and someone else breaks 3, 4. and 5, who's more perfect in God's eyes? Neither. One sin is just as bad as any other.

So, don't let the Pharisees get you down. We all need grace. You, me, your brother, your sister, your parents, your teachers, that bully at school, and yes, even Pharisees.

Thoughts to Ponder

What does God's grace mean to you?

Do you have a Pharisee in your life? What do you think is his or her motive in judging others?

Bumper Sticker for the Day

**Pharisees—someone with 20/20 vision for your faults
and legally blind for theirs.**

Scripture to Stand On

For whoever keeps the whole law and yet stumbles at just one point is guilty of breaking all of it. For he who said, "Do not commit adultery," also said, "Do not murder." If you do not commit adultery but do commit murder, you have become a lawbreaker.

JAMES 2:10-11

Hello Again, Lord ...

Lord, help me to follow your example and not let the Pharisees deter me from what you've called me to do.

Talk Show

Do you know someone who talks ... and talks ... and tallllllllll-llllllllllllks? You keep waiting for a chance to cut in, but he or she never gives it to you. People like this don't have conversations. They have monologues, and you're their audience of one.

Why do they do this? Why do they go on and on and on and on, without taking a single breath?

It could be that they're excited. Excited people tend to talk a lot. They can't really help it. They're thrilled with whatever is going on in their lives at this particular time.

Yet no one's excited 24-7, so if they're doing it day in and day out, chances are there's another reason for their monopolizing the conversation.

Perhaps they're nervous. Nervous people can talk a lot, too. They talk to hide their nervousness. Sometimes they're nervous because they don't know you that well, so they feel they have to cover up the discomfort of the moment. Or they're nervous because they don't know themselves that well and are unsure of the validity of their own opinions. So they talk and talk, hoping you won't challenge their belief systems.

Or maybe they're talking a lot because, well, they're rude and self-centered. They don't think you could possibly have anything to say that's as important as what they're contributing to the conversation. So they talk and talk and talk and never let you get a word in edgewise.

We can all overlook nervousness. We can put up with over-enthusiasm. But who wants to hang around someone who's rude and insensitive? I know I don't. And you probably don't either.

So the next time you're stuck in a one-way conversation with someone, try to analyze what it is that's making him or her talk so much. If it's excitement, nervousness, or some other harmless reason, go ahead and endure. But if that person is just being rude and self-centered, you might want to excuse yourself from the conversation. The talker might not even notice you've left, anyway.

Thoughts to Ponder

When you're having a conversation with your friends, who would you say talks the most?

How does it feel when you're with someone and he or she never takes a breath or lets you get a word in edgewise?

Bumper Sticker for the Day
**Those who don't listen seldom say anything
worth listening to.**

Scripture to Stand On

My dear brothers, take note of this: Everyone should be quick to listen, slow to speak and slow to become angry.

JAMES 1:19

Hello Again, Lord ...

Lord, help me to remember that if only one person does the talking, both sides miss out on a lot.

Flyin' High

Picture this: Two baby birds anxious to learn to fly. The father bird tells them to go to the north side of the nest. From there, they'll jump from the tree together, and as gravity pulls them toward the earth, they're to watch him and flap their wings the same way he does. They needn't worry, because he'll be there to fly under them and lift them up, should they run into any problems.

Excited, the young birds prepare for their flight. But as they're taking their places on the north side of the nest, the younger of the two birds happens to look down at the view from the south side of the nest.

"Whoa! Look at that!" he says, pointing out all the things that are on the south side. "Why's Dad taking us off the north side? This is the side with all the fun!"

"There are too many branches on this side of the nest," the older brother says. "It's too dangerous." But the younger bird doesn't listen. His father is taking too long and he doesn't want to wait.

He's tired of the nest. It's cramped and prickly and, can we say, b-o-r-i-n-g? There's a whole world out there to see, and he's determined to get started!

So he tells his brother of his plan, and while his father is out gathering worms for their breakfast, he boldly leaps off the south side of the tree and starts flapping his wings in an effort to fly.

And he flaps.

And he flaps.

And he flaps ... right into the first branch. SMACK! He hits it full force, tumbles off, and continues his descent.

Seeing the next branch beneath him, he tries to flap away from it, but he can't. SMACK! He slams right into it and then continues his fall. SMACK! He hits another branch. SMACK! And another one. Down he goes until he finally splashes into an old bucket full of water.

Gasping for breath, he flaps his way over to the side of the bucket. Feathers drenched and feeling a bit wobbly, he spits out a small fountain of water from his beak and looks upward toward his brother.

"Dad never said flying would be this hard," he says.

From across the field, his father sees him and flies to him.

"Climb onto my back," his father says.

When the little bird is safely on board, the father flies him back to the nest and tells him to wait there.

Now it's his brother's turn. The older brother climbs onto their dad's back and soon they're off. They fly high, they fly low, they do rollovers and loops and all sorts of fancy aviator tricks. Then finally, when the older brother feels sure enough, the father lets him fly on his own, but stays right by his side. The younger bird watches as his brother flaps and flaps and finally flies. Really flies!

When they return to the nest, the younger brother, who is still hurting from all his wounds, can't help but ask, "How can you make it look so easy, bro? I almost broke my neck out there!"

The older brother takes a moment to catch his breath from the exhilaration, then smiles,

"It's really not so hard when you do it Dad's way."

Thoughts to Ponder

Which do you identify with most, the younger brother or the older one?

If God is taking too long to let you fly on your own in a certain situation, do you think he might be saving you from learning something the hard way?

Bumper Sticker for the Day
Not everyone who's flapping is flying.
Some are in a tailspin.

Scripture to Stand On

Humble yourselves before the Lord, and he will lift you up.
JAMES 4:10

Hello Again, Lord ...

Help me to be patient, Lord, so that I can soar with you.

Choosing Sides

After the terrorist attacks on the World Trade Center in New York and the Pentagon in Washington, D.C., President George Bush vowed that the perpetrators of such barbaric acts, and those who harbor them, would suffer the consequences. He called upon the countries of the world to publicly choose sides. Were they for us or against us? There would be no more straddling of the fence. If they proclaimed to be against terrorism, they would need to publicly join the fight against it. They couldn't say one thing and do another. They would have to finally step up to the plate and be counted.

In these uncertain times, God is calling on us to also step up to the plate and be counted. No longer can we straddle the fence on faith issues. Are we on God's team, or are we against him?

For years we've gotten away with being complacent. We could wear our commitment to God one day and take it off the next. We could have our church friends and our school or work friends, and a different personality to go along with each.

But those days are over.

Our schools, our jobs, our government, and even our churches need to see more of us stepping up to the plate and choosing which side of the fence we're truly on. This isn't the time for lip service. If we're truly going to make a difference, a positive difference, in this world, we need to stand up and be counted. We need to proclaim our allegiance to God both in our safe havens and in all those places where we've been fence-straddling for far too long.

Thoughts to Ponder

Are there any areas of your life where you've been doing some fence-straddling?

Why do you think it's time you stop straddling fences when it comes to your faith in God?

Bumper Sticker for the Day
**It's impossible to get very far in life if you
never shift out of neutral.**

Scripture to Stand On

And the scripture was fulfilled that says, "Abraham believed God, and it was credited to him as righteousness," and he was called God's friend.
JAMES 2:23

Hello Again, Lord ...

Lord, I pledge to you my allegiance, both when it's easy and when it isn't.

Sheep Work

Do you know that preachers, evangelists, Sunday school teachers, youth pastors, and other teachers of God's Word have a responsibility that goes beyond showing up and delivering our lesson each week? Not only are preachers and teachers responsible to their church for what they say and do, but God is going to grade them on how seriously they took their assignment, too.

So does this mean they can never laugh? Of course not. Holy laughter is not only good, it's God-ordained. God ordains joy. He created each of us with the ability to laugh. He meant for us to do it as often as possible. And believe me, if anyone needs a good laugh, it's people in the ministry. With all the negativity that so often gets thrown their way, a couple of belly laughs a day can't hurt.

Pastors and teachers don't have to take themselves seriously, but they do have to take their calling seriously. They live under grace just like you and I, but because of their position, people look up to them. They watch their actions and give added weight to the words they speak. Without even realizing it, they can hurt feelings, seemingly ignore people, and be grossly misunderstood.

Yet we can do our share of hurting, too.

"How come he never plans anything fun?"
"She never lets us do what we want."
"His sermons are too long."
"Her voice is too scratchy."

"Do we have to sing the same song over and over and over again?"

We're never satisfied, are we?

Now, certainly, if a minister's behaving in a way that's not right, then we should bring that to his or her attention in a loving way. If he or she is setting a bad example, gossiping about families in the church, showing favoritism, doing the very things he or she teaches against, then that behavior needs to be discussed, but through the proper channels.

I once had a lady stop me in a busy mall and proceed to tell me how wrong her pastor had been in a certain situation. There was a long line of people standing well within hearing distance. I couldn't help but wonder what these people were thinking about our God at that particular moment. Would this woman's tirade have tempted the unchurched to start attending regularly? I seriously doubt it, but this lady was so concerned about her pastor's actions that she didn't even realize the damage her own actions might be doing.

Jesus said, "They will know you are my disciples by your love," not "by your nitpicking," not "by your judgmental attitudes," not "by your superior attitudes," not "by your 'words' of love." He said "by your love."

Sometimes we don't show a lot of love to those in authority over us, especially when they're not around to hear what we say about them. Yet we have to be careful. If our untamed tongue ends up discouraging a man or woman out of the ministry, God might put a few bad marks on our own report cards, too.

Thoughts to Ponder

Why do you think it's important to encourage your ministers?

Why do you think God said that more will be required of teachers and preachers?

Bumper Sticker for the Day
If you think sheep are easy to lead, why aren't there more shepherds in the world?

Scripture to Stand On

Not many of you should presume to be teachers, my brothers, because you know that we who teach will be judged more strictly.

JAMES 3:1

Hello Again, Lord ...

Lord, help me to encourage my pastor today. I might be the only one doing so.

A Broadway Debut

I'm all dressed up. At the Imperial Theater in New York City. In the heart of Broadway. I'm there to see the musical *Les Misérables*. It's a wonderful production. The cast is fantastic, the singing incredible, the story powerful and moving. I even lucked out and landed some great seats.

A night doesn't get any better than this.

Until ...

Intermission.

I go upstairs to visit the ladies' lounge. On my return, as I'm headed down the staircase, I get about three steps into the descent and ... tumble ... TUMMMMMMMMMMBLE . . . all the way down, landing in a heap at the landing.

A night doesn't get any more embarrassing than this.

I glance up, just long enough to see the pant legs of about four or five men standing around me, including a security guard. I hear a concerned, "Are you all right?" Then an, "Are you hurt?" followed by a, "Man, did you see that?" and an, "I saw it, but I don't believe it!"

I'm too embarrassed to elevate my glance past their knees, but I know from all the new legs standing around that a crowd has now gathered. I mumble something to the effect that, yes, I am alive, then I gather myself together and limp all the way back to my great seat about six rows from the stage.

My Broadway debut.

Have you ever made a scene like that where you wanted to crawl into a hole and disappear from public view? It happens to all of us. Man, woman, girl, boy, rich, poor, famous, and not so famous, everyone has moments in their life that they'd like to do over.

Unfortunately, we can't.

Yet we can survive those moments. How? By laughing about them. Moments like these do serve a very important purpose—they keep us humble.

And I'll always be able to say I made a lasting impression on Broadway.

Thoughts to Ponder

What was your most embarrassing moment?

When we can laugh about our embarrassing moments, it takes away their sting. Have you had a good laugh yet over your most embarrassing moment?

Bumper Sticker for the Day
Sometimes humble pie is the best dessert.

Scripture to Stand On

But he gives us more grace. That is why Scripture says: "God opposes the proud but gives grace to the humble."

JAMES 4:6

Hello Again, Lord ...

Lord, help me to remember that it's healthy to have a good laugh at myself once in a while.

Budgeting for Eternity

Aren't you glad they don't sell tickets to heaven on eBay? If eternal life were available only to the highest bidder, most of us would never be able to walk those streets of gold. Think about it—how much would eternal life go for? If mere paintings and jewelry can sell into the millions of dollars, how much would a guaranteed ticket to heaven cost us?

Oh, we might place a bid in the beginning, when the starting amount was at five dollars. We might even stick with the auction until it went up to forty or fifty dollars. Maybe even one hundred dollars. We could get a twenty-year advance on our allowance and even bid a thousand or two. Or we might even borrow against our college fund (if we have one) and pay five or ten thousand dollars. Yet we still wouldn't have a chance of winning the auction. There are plenty of people in this world who think of ten thousand dollars as petty cash. They'd outbid us so fast, our heads would spin and our computers would freeze up.

God knows that and, because he's fair, he's made heaven something that money can't buy. In fact, the love of money might even keep a few of us out of heaven.

Money may mean a lot in this life, but it means very little in the afterlife. Believe it or not, the things that make someone rich in heaven are going to be the very things that might have held people back here on earth. Kindness, consideration, sacrifice, meekness, peacefulness—none of these qualities seem like an asset in our do-anything-to-get-ahead society, but they mean everything in heaven.

Money isn't eternal. Just look in your wallet if you want to see how lasting money is. Chances are, what you had in there two weeks ago probably isn't in there now. Riches are fleeting. They'll pass. Yet what you've done for other people, what you've done for God, the eternal things you've done are what's going to count in heaven. Not your bank account.

Thoughts to Ponder

Do you think only rich people have to guard against greed?

List two or three things that you've done this year that have eternal value.

Bumper Sticker for the Day
Money may talk, but it can't talk its way into heaven.

Scripture to Stand On

But the one who is rich should take pride in his low position, because he will pass away like a wild flower.

JAMES 1:10

Hello Again, Lord ...

Lord, help me never to forget that for the biggest return on my dollar, I need to invest in eternity.

One Good Deed Deserves Another ...
and Another ... and Another

When the Bible says that faith without works is dead, don't misread that to mean that we have to earn our salvation. Because we can't. We can't possibly do enough good deeds to "earn" God's grace. That's why it's called grace. It's a gift we can't possibly earn.

In other words, if we serve 486 meals to the homeless, sing in six Christmas musicals and four Easter cantatas, help out with three consecutive Vacation Bible Schools, attend 3,496 youth meetings and twelve teen camps, and go caroling at five different convalescent homes every Christmas, we still can't earn grace. It simply cannot be bought.

Think about it—if our salvation was dependent on how much we could do for God, then why did Christ have to die on the cross? His sacrifice wouldn't have been necessary if we could do enough good deeds to earn our forgiveness on our own.

But Jesus did have to die. Grace had to be offered. It's up to us to accept it freely. But we can't earn it.

Does that mean, then, that we should never do good deeds? Of course not. Performing good deeds is our faith in action. It isn't the price of our faith. We don't do good deeds to get something (that would be manipulative). We don't do good deeds because we don't want to lose God's love (that would be fear). We do good deeds so that others will see God through us. It's to share our faith with them. For it's by our kindness that those around us will see the kindness of God. It's by the forgiveness we show others that others will see and seek the forgiveness of God.

Thoughts to Ponder

Think about the last good deed that you did. What do you think were your true motives behind it? A fear of God? Trying to earn his grace? Or was it because God has done so much for you?

Why do you think it's impossible to earn God's grace?

Bumper Sticker for the Day
Grace—the best travel agent for heaven.

Scripture to Stand On

You see that his faith and his actions were working together, and his faith was made complete by what he did.

JAMES 2:22

Hello Again, Lord ...

Lord, I wish I could be good enough to deserve your love, but I'm so grateful that I don't have to be.

Spiritual Selfishness

As a child you were probably taught to share. If your little brother wanted half of your brownie, you no doubt had to give it to him. Or at least give him a taste of it. When your family visited amusement parks, I'm sure the ride operators didn't let you stay on the roller coaster as long as you wanted. You had to get off and let someone else enjoy it for a while. To hog all the fun at an amusement park or eat the last crumb of a brownie in front of your little brother would be selfish, right?

Do you know, when it comes to God, we sometimes get a little selfish, too? We don't invite our school friends to church because, well, those are our church friends and we don't really want to share them. Or we quickly change the subject when someone starts asking us about spiritual matters because we already know the Lord, and there are so many other things to talk about.

One thing that came out of the devastating day of terror in New York City and Washington, D.C. was the news that shortly after the incidents, Bible sales doubled. People were looking for hope in the midst of the hopelessness they were feeling. Their world was in a scary whirlwind of change, and they were looking to God for answers.

When our friends ask us about God, do we pretend we don't hear them and keep all the peace to ourselves? Do we hog all the hope?

Or are we sharing?

Thoughts to Ponder

Would you say you tend to keep God to yourself or do you share his message of hope?

Do you think more people are looking for spiritual answers today?

Bumper Sticker for the Day
When it comes to God, every day is Share Day.

Scripture to Stand On

Remember this: Whoever turns a sinner from the error of his way will save him from death and cover over a multitude of sins.

JAMES 5:20

Hello Again, Lord ...

Lord, help me to remember that you were never intended to be a secret.

The "Prayer Request"

Hmmm, another scripture about the tongue. Some years ago I went to the funeral of a friend of mine. This lady was in her seventies and could have been anyone's grandmother. She was sweet, kind, and gentle. I don't think I ever heard her say an unkind word about anyone.

At her funeral, though, I noticed that the word "God" was missing from the eulogy and the entire funeral, for that matter. It seemed strange to me. After all, most funerals have God and heaven as the central point of the message.

Afterward, I mentioned this to some friends of mine to see if anyone else had noticed the absence of God in the funeral proceedings.

"It was her dying request," one lady explained.

What?! Why would anyone make a deathbed request like that? Why would she choose to leave God out of her funeral when she was getting ready to meet him? I knew this lady wasn't an atheist, so I wondered what horrible thing had happened to her that had caused such bitterness against God.

They told me.

Evidently, some thirty or forty years before, this woman and her daughter (who had become pregnant out of wedlock) had been gossiped about by the people in her church. She never forgave them, and she never forgave God. The lady went to her grave bitter, hurt, and apparently quite confused. It wasn't God who had gossiped about her. It was his people.

Maybe that's one reason why God hates gossip. He gets blamed for a lot of it.

So then why do Christians gossip? Often it's to get the attention off their own shortcomings. If they can point out the faults (or invent faults) of others, then it makes them feel better about the things they do.

Sometimes they might even spin gossip as a "prayer request." They pretend to be concerned about a situation, then gladly share every sordid detail of that situation. Yet God is not fooled. Gossip is gossip is gossip. Apparently, Christians were pulling this same trick back in the Bible days. Why else would so many scriptures deal with the subject of gossip?

God knows when we're secretly happy that someone is having a problem. He knows when we're dying to make that third, fourth, and fifth telephone call to get the word out so everyone can know ... I mean, "pray." He knows our hearts. We can't fool him. And if we truly love those around us as we say we do, then we will handle their personal difficulties the same way we'd want them to handle ours—with discretion, compassion, and private prayers to God.

Thoughts to Ponder

Have you ever found yourself sharing gossip under the guise of a "prayer request"?

Has anyone ever gossiped about you under the guise of "helping"? How did it make you feel?

Bumper Sticker for the Day
**When God said, "Be still and know that I am God,"
he was talking to our tongues, too.**

Scripture to Stand On

All kinds of animals, birds, reptiles and creatures of the sea are being tamed and have been tamed by man, but no man can tame the tongue. It is a restless evil, full of deadly poison.

JAMES 3:7-8

Hello Again, Lord ...

Lord, help me to remember to take the private matters of my friends to you, instead of to the world.

Quick-Change Artist

Wouldn't it be nice if we could change the minute we wanted to?

"Could you please stop doing that?" someone would say.

"Oh, I'm so sorry," we'd answer. "Why, of course, I'll cease doing it immediately. I hope I haven't caused you any undue discomfort."

That'd be great, wouldn't it? No struggle. No returning to old habits. Simple as that. One word and we'd promptly stop our argumentative, prideful, envious, gossipy, resentful, unhealthy behavior.

OK, now back to the real world. Life doesn't happen like that. Change is a process. Sometimes slower than others, but it takes time. There's no getting around it.

True, the Bible says that when we give our hearts to the Lord, we are new creatures in him. But bad behaviors are learned behaviors and sometimes it takes a little longer to notify our personality of a spiritual change. Not to worry, though, God is patient. He always sees the good in us, even if it takes a little while for that good to rise to the surface so the rest of the world can see it.

Because of this, those around us may get impatient, waiting for us to start acting differently. If they see even a glimpse of the old character, they might start discounting that new leaf we say we turned over.

"Look at that!" they might say. "He's acting just like he's always acted!" Or, "Listen to her! Can you believe that language? Obviously, she hasn't changed a bit!"

Don't get discouraged by impatient onlookers. Keep doing your best. Keep allowing God to change you, minute by minute, hour by hour, day by day. The fact of the matter is that each one of us is a work in progress. God won't be through working on us until we take that first step into heaven. So be patient with yourself. God is.

Thoughts to Ponder

In what ways would you say you're a work in progress?

Why do you think change doesn't always take place overnight?

Bumper Sticker for the Day
Change is a process that even failure can't stop ... unless we let it.

Scripture to Stand On

Judgment without mercy will be shown to anyone who has not been merciful.

JAMES 2:13a

Hello Again, Lord ...

Lord, help me to show mercy to others. And to myself.

A Yes Man

How dependable should our word be? God tells us here in James how he wants it to be. He says that our "yes" should be "yes" and our "no" should be "no." Not much wiggle room, is there?

So does this mean we can't ever change our mind? Of course not. Sometimes we might find ourselves in a position where we've said yes to something we shouldn't be doing in the first place, because it's wrong. In a situation like this, God would want us to change our mind, and the sooner the better.

What God is saying here is that when we make a promise to someone, we need to live up to our word. When we say we'll help out with our church drama group, we need to show up at the rehearsals, not just the performance. When we tell our parents we're going to the mall, we shouldn't go to our friend's house instead. When we say we'll have that science project in by Friday, we need to have it in by Friday, even if it means missing our favorite television show. God wants us to be people who can be trusted. People of our word.

But hey, he's God. Why on earth would he care if I get my science project in on time?

God cares because if we lose the trust of those around us, they won't pay much attention when we talk about him. In other words, our witness won't mean much because our word won't mean much.

Yet if we fulfill our promises, if we do what we say we're going to do, if we don't let other people down, if we go where we're supposed to go and do what we're supposed to do, then our witness will have credibility. People will listen when we want to tell them about the Lord. People will trust that what we're telling them about God is true, instead of treating it as just another one of our broken promises.

Thoughts to Ponder

Would you say you're a person of your word?

In what areas of your life do you think you need to become more dependable?

Bumper Sticker for the Day
Broken promises are the hardest break to repair.

Scripture to Stand On

Above all, my brothers, do not swear—not by heaven or by earth or by anything else. Let your "Yes" be yes, and your "No," no, or you will be condemned.

JAMES 5:12

Hello Again, Lord ...

Lord, thank you for always keeping your promises. Help me to do likewise.

School of Higher Learning

If I could give you one word of advice on how to live your life, it would be this: Remain teachable.

One of these days you're going to walk across the platform of your high school or college and be handed a diploma. Your school years will be behind you, and you'll find yourself traveling full speed ahead into the adult world. It's an exciting time and a natural progression of life.

What they won't give you, though, is a diploma in life. For most of us, that comes much later.

So, what's a "life diploma"? It's what you get at the end of your days. It's not tangible, of course. It's not something your heirs can frame and hang on their wall. It's just an inner satisfaction in knowing you've accomplished everything you were meant to accomplish during your time here on this earth. It's knowing you didn't waste a minute of it. You met life's challenges, and didn't run from them. Your faith survived whatever discouragements came your way. And you remained teachable.

Too often after we leave school, we think there's nothing left to learn. We've collected the right number of credits, passed all the necessary courses, and the diploma that we're now holding in our hands attests to the fact that we know it all, everything there is to know.

Obviously, nothing could be further from the truth. We have plenty more to learn, and the only way to do it is to be teachable.

If we're teachable, it won't matter how many failures we have to go through, because we know we can learn something from each one. If we're teachable, we'll never stop having new knowledge to share with others. If we're teachable, we'll always be improving ourselves. If we're teachable, we'll humbly look to God for our answers.

Want to know the secret to finishing life well? Remain teachable.

Thoughts to Ponder

Would you say you have a teachable spirit?

Why do you think life is easier for those who are teachable?

Bumper Sticker for the Day
**Learning is like your heartbeat.
It is meant to continue as long as you do.**

Scripture to Stand On

Perseverance must finish its work so that you may be mature and complete, not lacking anything.

JAMES 1:4

Hello Again, Lord ...

Lord, help me pass the school of life.

The Enemy Is Us

Unfortunately, Christians have a reputation for shooting their wounded. When fellow believers slip, instead of reaching out to them, holding them up, encouraging them, and believing the best about them, we tend to step on their fingers while they dangle on the ledge, discourage them, and jump to the worst possible conclusion at the slightest suspicion of impropriety.

But wait a minute—didn't Jesus say that people would know that we're his disciples by the love we show each other?

Oops.

You mean we're not supposed to add our two cents worth concerning the situation?

Oops.

We're not supposed to stand up on our soapbox and state our disapproval of the fallen soldier's behavior?

Oops.

We're not supposed to use these people as an example, publicly humiliate them, then have what's left of their reputations for dessert after church?

You mean that's not how we're supposed to act?

No.

Look at how Christ acted when people tried to put the law over grace.

Remember the woman caught in adultery: "If any one of you is without sin, let him be the first to throw a stone at her."

The woman with the alabaster box: The disciples complained that she should have let them sell the ointment and give the money to the poor, instead of "wasting" it by pouring it on Jesus' head.

His reply: "Why are you bothering this woman? She has done a beautiful thing to me. The poor you will always have with you, but you will not always have me."

The repentant thief on the cross: "I tell you the truth, today you will be with me in paradise."

The gospel is about grace. It's about restoration. It's about forgiveness. It's about an imperfect people and a perfect God. It's about caring for our wounded, not finishing them off.

Thoughts to Ponder

How do you react when you hear a fellow soldier of faith has taken a "hit"?

Why do you think it's important for us to rally around each other in moments of crisis, instead of "shooting our wounded"?

Bumper Sticker for the Day
**Those who deny others an ounce of grace
deny themselves a pound.**

Scripture to Stand On

There is only one Lawgiver and Judge, the one who is able to save and destroy. But you—who are you to judge your neighbor?

JAMES 4:12

Hello Again, Lord ...

Lord, may I show mercy for another's mistakes, so you'll show mercy for mine.

Bad Hair Day

Ever have one of those days where everything that can possibly go wrong does go wrong? As far as you can tell, it's the worst day of your week. Your month. Your year. Maybe even the worst day of your life. You wonder if anyone has ever had a day as bad as the one you're having.

Well, believe it or not, someone did have a worse day. In fact, his day was probably the worst day for anyone in history. The man's name was Job, and the Bible tells us all about his bad day.

You see, Job was a blessed man. He had a whole bunch of children (three daughters and seven sons, to be exact). He also owned seven thousand sheep, three thousand camels, five hundred yoke of oxen, and five hundred donkeys, and had a large number of servants. He was a millionaire even without Regis Philbin's help.

Yes, everything seemed to be going great in Job's life, until this one particular day when everything started to fall apart. What's worse, none of it was his fault.

The Bible tells us that one day when Job's children were feasting (hanging out, scarfing down pizza and all-you-can-eat chips and dip—you get the idea) at the oldest brother's house, a messenger came to Job and told him that the Sabeans had attacked and had stolen all his oxen and killed all his servants except the one speaking.

That was a lot of oxen. And servants. Bummer.

But then, while he was still speaking, another messenger

came and said that fire had fallen from the sky and burned up all his sheep and the servants who were with them. Only that one messenger escaped with his life.

Job's bad day wasn't over yet.

While that messenger was speaking, another one arrived. (If I were Job, I think I would have quit answering the door by now!) This messenger told him that the Chaldeans had formed three raiding parties and had come in and stolen all his camels and killed the servants with them.

Then another messenger came and told Job that a mighty wind had hit the house where his children were partying, killing all of them.

How's that for a bad day?

But what was Job's response in the midst of all these calamities?

"Naked I came from my mother's womb, and naked I will depart. The Lord gave and the Lord has taken away, may the name of the Lord be praised." The Bible also says that, "In all this, Job did not sin by charging God with wrongdoing."

When things go wrong in our lives, we often want to blame God. Yet, while God may have allowed these things to happen, as he did in Job's case, he didn't cause them.

Job didn't cause them either. The Bible says that Job was a righteous man. Some people think that trouble comes into someone's life because of something he or she has done wrong. Job even had a few of these kind of people in his life. They came to him in the midst of his trouble and assured him that everything that was happening to him must be because of some sin he had committed.

Now granted, if we do wrong, we can certainly bring consequences on ourselves. Yet the fact that we have problems or illness in our lives doesn't mean that we've done anything to deserve it. Job was a person who was "blameless in God's sight," and he still had problems.

Yet, what happened to Job after this period of loss? God restored everything he had lost and blessed him with more than he had at the beginning. Job ended up with fourteen thousand sheep (he had lost seven thousand, remember?), six thousand camels (he had lost three thousand), one thousand yoke of oxen, and one thousand donkeys (he had lost five hundred of each), and God also gave him more children (seven more sons and three more daughters).

Job went through a tough time in his life, but he trusted God. Job trusted, despite the discouragement he received from "well-meaning people." Job trusted, despite the appearance of his circumstances. Job trusted, despite his human weaknesses. Job trusted God, and God did not let him down.

Thoughts to Ponder

When things go wrong in your life, where do you tend to put the blame?

What do you think Job learned from his "bad day"? What do you think you can learn from your "bad days"?

Bumper Sticker for the Day
If God is the only one in your corner, that's enough.

Scripture to Stand On

You have heard of Job's perseverance and have seen what the Lord finally brought about.

JAMES 5:11b

Hello Again, Lord ...

When things go wrong, help me to remember that I still belong to you.

What Counts

After the World Trade Center and Pentagon terrorist attacks, most of us reevaluated what was really important in life. Suddenly it didn't matter whether or not we got those new shoes, that new dress, or attended Friday night's party. We didn't care if we won the cheerleader tryouts or made the football team.

As a matter of fact, many of the things that normally occupied our time and attention slipped away from our consciousness and were replaced by things like family, friends, and faith. Nothing else seemed as important. Even MTV stopped showing music videos and just talked about the happenings of the day. Everyone was searching for answers, for a little stability, for hope.

It's unfortunate that it took a national disaster to remind us what life is all about. Life isn't about how much we can accumulate or the latest song climbing to the top of the Billboard charts. It's not about the hairstyles or our appetite for movie star gossip. Life is about loving each other, it's about bravery in the face of insurmountable odds, and it's about faith and thankfulness.

After the disaster, Bible sales went through the roof. Suddenly going to church didn't seem like such a sacrifice, and most of us freely talked about God to anyone who would listen. It didn't seem out of place anymore. In fact, everyone seemed to want to talk about God.

It's funny, but when things go along smoothly, it's easy to

forget about God. We know he's a part of our lives, but we don't really talk to him as often as we should.

But when we need him, when nothing around us is making any sense, when we're frightened and forced to admit we're dependent on him, that's when we bring him into the forefront of our lives.

I have a feeling he'd like to be in the forefront in the good times, too.

Thoughts to Ponder

How did the events of 9-11 change your thinking about what's important in life?

Do you find it easier now to talk to your friends about God?

Bumper Sticker for the Day
God—where is he in the middle of a crisis?
The same place he was before—right beside you.

Scripture to Stand On

Consider it pure joy, my brothers, whenever you face trials of many kinds, because you know that the testing of your faith develops perseverance.

JAMES 1:2-3

Hello Again, Lord ...

Lord, thank you for always being there whenever I've called on you, and forgive me for the times when you've been there and I've ignored you.

No Easy Job

It's hard being a father when no matter what you do for your kids, it never seems to be enough.

It's hard being a father when you get that desperate call letting you know that she's in trouble. You rush to her aid again, all the while wondering why children always have to learn things the hard way.

It's hard being a father when your child asks for something and even though you'd like to give it to him, you remember he hasn't thanked you for the last ten things you've given him.

It's hard being a father when your children tune you out.

It's hard being a father when your children are disrespectful.

It's hard being a father when it seems the only time your kid talks to you is when she wants something.

It's hard being a father when your child asks for your advice, but then he still goes ahead and does his own thing.

It's hard being a father when you have sacrificed so much for your kids and they take it all so lightly, if they even notice at all.

It's hard being a father when you tell your child to hold your hand, but instead she pulls away.

It's hard being a father when you want your child to just sit and talk, but he's got too many things to do and too many places to go.

It's hard being a father when your child acts embarrassed of you.

It's hard being a father when your child rejects you and runs away, and you know you won't rest until he's safe in your arms again.

It's hard being a father. Just ask God.

Thoughts to Ponder

What kind of son or daughter do you think you've been to God?

What kind of father do you think he is to you?

Bumper Sticker for the Day
God—the indisputable Father of the Year.

Scripture to Stand On

He chose to give us birth through the word of truth, that we might be a kind of firstfruits of all he created.

JAMES 1:18

Hello Again, Lord ...

Lord, forgive me for the times when I've acted like a brat. Thank you for loving me anyway.

He Loves Me, He Loves Me Not

In preparation for my marriage, I had to send away for my birth certificate. I had always celebrated my birthday on September 2, so you can imagine my surprise when I received the certificate and discovered that it said September 1 instead! For eighteen years it was the second of September, and now all of a sudden I was going to have to start celebrating it a day earlier. To this day, the first still doesn't "feel" right.

I suppose someone could try to convince me that my mother didn't really care enough about me to notice the day I was born. But I know better. I'm so confident of how much my mother loved me that doubts of this kind don't even enter my mind. Why? Because of the sacrifices she made for her family over the years, because of the care she showed, and because she told me she loved me.

Sometimes people try to convince us that God doesn't love or care for us.

"If God really loved you, he wouldn't be making you go through this situation."

"If God cared for you, he would have prevented your broken heart."

"If God loved you, he'd make all your dreams come true."

I hope you know better. I hope you're so confident of how much God loves you that those kinds of doubts don't even enter your mind. You may not understand everything that's going on in your life right now, but don't ever doubt God's love. Life is full of change and unpredictability. Yet that one fact is unshakable.

Thoughts to Ponder

Has anyone ever tried to make you doubt God's love for you?

God proved his love for you by giving his son to die on a cross in your place. Do you think that was sufficient proof to forever convince you of his love?

Bumper Sticker for the Day
Faith shouts in the face of doubts.

Scripture to Stand On

Don't be deceived, my dear brothers.

JAMES 1:16

Hello Again, Lord ...

Lord, help me to have unshakable faith in your unshakable love.

Amazing!

How do we know that God is a God of grace? By how readily he forgives us. Notice that I didn't say easily. Our orgiveness didn't come easy. Its price tag was the cross. But God freely and readily gives his grace to whoever asks for it. And we're not talking about that conditional, superficial human kind of forgiveness, that "All right, I forgive you, but if I ever hear of you doing anything like that again, don't come crawling back to me" kind of grace. God's grace is true grace, his forgiveness is genuine. That's why they call it amazing.

God's grace is waiting for you when you least deserve it.

God's grace is waiting for you when you don't expect it.

God's grace is waiting for you when others aren't offering it to you.

God's grace is waiting for you when you don't think you need it.

God's grace is waiting for you when you're too ashamed to reach for it.

God's grace is waiting for you when you think there is no hope.

God's grace is waiting for you when you think it's too late.

God's grace is waiting for you while you're trying everything else.

God's grace will free you.

God's grace will change you.

God's grace will strengthen you.

God's grace will enlighten you.

God's grace will be your hope.

God's grace will be your encouragement
God's grace will be your salvation.
God's grace will amaze you.

Thoughts to Ponder

How does it make you feel to know that God is ready to forgive you right now?

Why do you think God's grace is so amazing?

Bumper Sticker for the Day
No matter how big the mess, one coat of grace still covers it.

Scripture to Stand On

If he has sinned, he will be forgiven.

JAMES 5:15b

Hello Again, Lord ...

Lord, thank you for your amazing grace.